THE COMPLETE GUIDE TO MUTTS

Selection, Care and Celebration from Puppyhood to Senior

Margaret H. Bonham

HOWELL
BOOK
HOUSE

In loving memory of the following mutts: Conan, Spice, Cuawn, Skye, Lightning, Mirin, Ed, Kersel, Jasmine, and Dancer; and purebreds Winnie, Quinn, and Shadow.

Especially in memory of Snopeak Kiana of Sky Warrior CGC, NA, U-AGI, WPD, WTD, PDX, A-PDX, my best friend. Miss you, Hoot.

And to Larry, Mom, and Dad, who encourage me.

• •

Howell Book House
Published by Wiley Publishing, Inc., Hoboken, New Jersey
Published simultaneously in Canada

For general information about our other products and services, please contact our Customer Care Department within the United States at (800) 762-2974, outside the United States at (317) 572-3993 or fax (317) 572-4002.

Wiley also publishes its books in a variety of electronic formats. Some content that appears in print may not be available in electronic books. For more information about Wiley products, visit our web site at www.wiley.com.

Library of Congress Cataloging-in-Publication Data:

Bonham, Margaret H.
  The complete guide to mutts/Margaret Bonham.
      p. cm.
Includes bibliographical references and index.
  ISBN 0-7645-4973-1 (alk. paper)
  1. Mutts (Dogs) I. Title.
  SF427.B622 2004
  636.7—dc22
                                        2003019495

Printed in the United States of America

10 9 8 7 6 5 4 3 2 1

CONTENTS

ACKNOWLEDGMENTS

A huge thanks to the following people (in no particular order):

- Jessica Faust, my agent, and Jackie Sach, her partner.
- Phyllis DeGioia, Karen Derrico and Kim Thornton for use of their stories.
- The Intermountain Humane Society for allowing me to photograph their dogs.
- Jessica Faust and Sadie; Karen Derrico and Barney, Phyllis DeGioia and Fred; Ginger, Berkley and Bruiser; Kathy and Jim Stabler and Robyn and Buddy; Mary Elyn Bigos and Boo and Lucky; Rhonda Metzger and Pepper Jubilation; and Maggie Meleski and Zoe for the photos.
- Dale Cunningham (Executive Editor) and Beth Adelman (editor and personal friend).
- Larry Bonham and Betty and Al Holowinski, who provide moral support.
- All the mutts who taught me something: Conan, Ed, Kersel, Skye, Spice, Lightning, Jasmine, Mirin, Rigel, Houston, and a host of others.
- My friends on DOGWRITERS-L (in case I miss someone below).
- Steve Dale, Deb Eldredge, Liz Palika, Bernd Gunter, Su Ewing, Dana Mackonis, and Cheryl Smith for their suggestions on famous mutts.

• •

CHAPTER 1

MIXING IT UP

THE MOST POPULAR DOG IN AMERICA

Meet the mutt. Sometimes maligned and unloved, sometimes exalted. The mutt, or mixed breed, has been around since the beginning of *Canis lupus familias,* when some wolves threw in their lot with humans.

You may be surprised to learn that the mutt is the most popular dog in the United States. The number of mixed breeds outnumbers any single AKC purebred and outnumbers or comes close to the numbers of all AKC purebred dogs combined. Fifty-one percent of all dog-owning households have at least one mixed breed dog. That makes roughly 20.4 million households with a mutt.

"People who have a mutt can't afford or don't want a purebred," says Karen Derrico, author of *Unforgettable Mutts.* "People are attracted to mutts because of their hardier reputation and their individualism. When you get a purebred, you know pretty much what you get, but there's a certain mystery to the mutt. You're getting a one-of-a-kind."

Most people would agree. America is the melting pot of various nations and cultures. The mutt can be considered the quintessential American dog.

"What breed is he?" is the most common question mutt owners hear. Many respond, "He's just a mutt." Just a mutt? Some of the most famous dogs were "just" mutts. If you look at literature, dogs like White Fang and Buck (from *Call of the Wild*) were mixed breeds. In cartoons, the lowly mutt is celebrated: Edgar and Farley in *For Better or for Worse,* Daisy in *Blondie,* Dogbert in *Dilbert,* Pluto in *Mickey Mouse,* Snert in *Hagar the Horrible,* Dogzilla in *The Buckets,* Odie in *Garfield* and Otto in *Beetle Bailey.*

DERRICO

People are attracted to mutts because of their hardier reputation and their individualism. This is Karen Derrico's mutt, Barney.

Phyllis DeGioia, mutt owner extraordinaire and freelance dog writer and editor, says, "Mutts are special because they are truly one of a kind; you won't be able to find another just like it. Their uniqueness is one of their most attractive qualities. It's the ultimate in rare breeds because, for the most part, you can't reproduce the mix—mostly because you don't know what it is."

Phyllis tells heart-wrenching stories about her own mutts, Fred and Ginger. Phyllis had just lost her beloved dog and told her veterinarian she wanted another dog. She received a phone call the same day.

"Fred was in the hospital when I met him. His legs were covered in vomit. When I sat next to him—a total stranger—he put his head on

Fred, a Westie-Bichon mix, is owned by Phyllis DeGioia.

my knee and looked at me. And that was it. He is now a therapy dog."
Fred had swallowed a Super Ball and, rather than pay for the surgery,
his owners had given him up to be either euthanized or placed with
another family. That family was Phyllis.

"Ginger appealed to me because the people who were giving her
away just drove her over and let her out of the car. She jumped out,
dragging a red leash, ran up the porch steps where I was sitting, into my
lap, and starting licking my face. Done deal in three seconds." Such is
the power of the mutt!

Mixed Reviews—What It Means to Bring a Mutt Into Your Life

Bringing a mutt—or any dog—into your life is a decision you should
not make lightly. In many cases, a dog is a 10- to 15-year commitment.
Will you be able to take care of a pet for all those 15 years? That will
include feeding, playing with, exercising and grooming your dog every
day. You will have to ensure that he is healthy by taking him to the veterinarian regularly for a health check and vaccinations. You will have to
bring him to the veterinarian when he is sick. You will have to clean up
after him, provide a stable environment where he can't be hurt or get
out and become lost, and you will have to provide for his basic needs:
food, water and a place to eliminate.

Ginger, a terrier mix, is owned by Phyllis DeGioia.

Surprisingly, many people equate the purchase price of a pet with the actual cost of dog ownership. Nothing could be further from the truth! There's no such thing as a free dog. When you consider the cost of veterinary care, daily food, supplies and the cost of your time, every dog is a very expensive companion indeed.

But there are benefits as well as costs. Bringing a mutt home means having a companion who is happy to see you every day. When the world is against you, your mutt will be there ready for you to pour your soul out to him. If your mutt is big, he can be a deterrent to criminals; if he is small, you may have a shopping companion or a pal you can take wherever you go. If your mutt is athletic, he can share your enthusiasm for sports and even introduce you to exciting sports such as agility or flyball.

We Don't Need No Stinkin' Pedigree

It may surprise you to learn that all dogs have pedigrees. It's true! From the highfalutin winner of the Westminster Kennel Club Dog Show to the dog you see raiding garbage cans on trash day, every dog has a pedigree.

What is a pedigree, you might ask. A pedigree is a listing of ancestry. That means if your dog had ancestors (a mother, father, grandparents, etc.), he has a pedigree. It may be an *unknown* pedigree, but every mutt has a pedigree.

So what does a pedigree mean? It depends largely on the dogs in the pedigree. Some dogs have impressive ancestors who won dog show championships or earned obedience, tracking, agility or herding titles. The pedigree establishes that the dog with those particular ancestors might have those same talents. But if this owner is unwilling to work toward those titles, that dog is no more valuable than your mutt. In fact, some mutts, such as Alaskan Huskies, are more valuable than purebred dogs.

Working Mutts—The Alaskan Husky Sled Dog

Which brings us to the subject of performance dogs. A group of mutts, sometimes referred to as a breed, are the Alaskan Huskies, who often compete in sled dog competitions.

What is an Alaskan Husky sled dog? Well, they are pedigreed mutts. They are dogs who come from established bloodlines that can be traced back to kennels that took Native American and Inuit dogs and bred them for racing. Over time, mushers (sled dog drivers) added various breeds into the Alaskan Husky lines. These add-ins included Greyhounds, Labrador Retrievers, Golden Retrievers, Border Collies, Irish Setters, Dalmatians, Borzoi, Salukis, Gordon Setters, German Shorthaired Pointers, Siberian Huskies, Alaskan Malamutes, Samoyeds, English Pointers and even wolf hybrids.

In the Alaskan Husky, there are two distinct types: hounds and huskies. The huskies look typically like Northern breeds, while the hounds tend to be slimmer and racier. Mushers may choose either, depending on their preferences and how they use their dogs.

Alaskan Huskies typically have some very elaborate pedigrees, many going back 10 generations or more. These sled dogs may cost anywhere from hundreds to thousands of dollars, depending on the bloodlines and the person selling the dogs. For example, a dog from an Iditarod-winning kennel may cost thousands of dollars, while a local dog may cost a few hundred or may even be free.

Alaskan Huskies may well be the best canine athletes. They've proven themselves capable of running over 1,000 miles in less than nine days, while eating the equivalent of 25 times an average person's daily diet. They're able to run 100 miles or more a day and enjoy doing it. In sprint races, many Alaskan Huskies are able to run 25 miles per

Sweetie is an Alaskan Husky, a type of mixed breed made for sled dog racing. She is owned by the author.

hour or more for six to 12 miles. Most purebreds can't match their speed or versatility.

Obedience, Agility and Other Performance Events

You may be surprised to learn that mixed breed dogs earn titles in competitive events such as obedience, agility, flyball and flying disc. Indeed, in many areas mutts excel in competition over their purebred counterparts. Mutts are among the top dogs in flying disc and flyball, competing against purebreds. Mutts do well in agility trials sponsored by UKC, USDAA and NADAC. They also compete against purebred dogs in obedience trials in UKC and AMBOR events. (Do all those organizations look like alphabet soup to you? Have a look in Appendix A, where I have sorted it all out.)

Robyn, a Cocker-Golden mix, negotiates a seesaw in an agility course.

Founders of New Breeds

Not surprisingly, mutts have become the foundation for new breeds. Indeed, it's hard to determine precisely when a group of dogs collectively becomes a "breed," except when they're recognized by an official kennel club such as the American Kennel Club (AKC) or the United Kennel Club (UKC). Most founders of breeds discover one or two individual dogs who they consider the ideal type for a particular job, and carefully select other dogs within the region who look similiar. Breeds such as the Labrador Retriever, the Alaskan Malamute and the Keeshond were developed in this manner.

In some cases, such as the Chinook and the Alaskan Klee Kai, the founding dog was a particular mutt who caught the eye of a breeder. The breeder then bred other dogs with this single dog to produce offspring who would become the foundation stock for a new breed.

From the Wrong Side of the Tracks—Famous Mixed Breeds

The most famous dogs aren't purebred—they're mutts! With the versatility and intelligence we see in mixed breeds, little wonder that mutts have often taken center stage. Take a look at some of the most famous mixed breeds:

- **Balto:** In 1925, when a diphtheria epidemic threatened the population of Nome, Alaska, mushers raced to bring the vaccine from Anchorage, nearly 1,000 miles away. Gunnar Kaasen's lead dog, Balto, is known for leading his team through a blinding storm and −70°F temperatures. The relay made the long trip in just six days. Balto was not a purebred Husky, as some people think, but rather a mixed breed dog imported from Norway.

- **Mut:** Costarred with Charlie Chaplin in the 1918 film *A Dog's Life*.

- **Laika:** Laika was the first living Earth creature in space. A mutt of indeterminate origins, Laika sadly paid for her fame with her life. Other mutts followed Laika to fame, and were safely recovered.

- **Spike:** Spike, aka Old Yeller, was a yellow flop-eared pup whom trainer Frank Weatherwax adopted from the Van Nuys Animal Shelter. Most famous for his role in the movie *Old Yeller,* Spike had sons who also starred in various motion pictures.

- **Fido:** Abraham Lincoln's dog was a midsize mutt and was the first presidential dog ever to have his photo taken.

- **Chinook:** Arthur Walden's famous lead sled dog, who later became the founder of the Chinook breed, was a mixed breed of Inuit Dog, German Shepherd Dog, Saint Bernard or another purebred.

- **Benji:** This lovable mutt has made his way into the hearts of millions in feature films. *Benji* is ranked as one of the Top 20 Must-See Movies for children by *People* magazine.

- **Murray:** Starred in the television series *Mad About You* from 1992 to 1999.

- **Freeway:** Starred in the television series *Hart to Hart* from 1979 to 1984.

- **Scruffy:** Starred with Hope Lange in the television series *The Ghost and Mrs. Muir* from 1968 to 1970.

- **Skip:** One of President Theodore Roosevelt's favorite dogs; Teddy found him on a bear hunt.

This list is by no means complete. No doubt, you can think of other famous mutts and mutts who do extraordinary things.

CHAPTER 2

• •

A HISTORY MYSTERY

Where did mixed breeds come from? Were there purebreds before there were mutts, or vice versa? What do we really know about mutts? Are there similarities among certain mixed breeds?

The answers are surprising.

CHICKEN OR THE EGG? MIXED OR PUREBRED?

Genetic research proves that all dogs evolved from *Canis lupus*, the wolf. That means the tiny Chihuahua, the huge Scottish Deerhound and everything in between came from the wolf. But how did dogs genetically become purebred as opposed to mixed breed? Well, that topic is the subject of much debate and conjecture.

According to much-publicized DNA and RNA analysis, the dog threw in her lot with humans somewhere between 60,000 and 125,000 years ago—about the same time humans started their migration out of Africa. This analysis has been hotly contested, because there isn't any conclusive fossilized evidence of dogs much beyond 20,000 years ago (note the gap).

In his book *Dogs,* Ray Coppinger proposes that there were some very clever wolves 15,000 to 20,000 years ago who knew a good thing when they saw it and decided to hang out with humans around the garbage dumps looking for free handouts. The wolves who were daring enough to raid Og's garbage were less cagey around humans than other wolves.

Regardless of whether you believe Coppinger's theories that the dog domesticated herself, eventually Og got used to the wolves—who started looking less like wolves and more like dogs, showing juvenile characteristics (neoteny—a fancy word), enabling them to regard humans as their pack members. At some point, Og thought these dogs might be useful for guarding or hunting. Current DNA studies suggest that all dogs can be traced back to a single group of canines in eastern Asia around 15,000 years ago.

What does all this mean? At one point, there was no such thing as purebred dogs because all dogs were the same—you could call them purebred or mutts, depending on how you look at things.

As Og and Ogina noticed, some dogs were better than other dogs at doing certain things. They chose to breed dogs who were better at doing those things. Dogs began to specialize. Those dogs eventually became purebreds.

We know there were purebred dogs as far back as ancient Egypt (and even further). Malamutes, Huskies, Pharaoh Hounds, Basenjis, Chow Chows, Dingos and Carolina Dogs are breeds whose ancestries predate historical records. How pure these breeds were kept depended largely on the humans and the availability of other breeding stock. We really don't know what prehistoric humans did when one dog accidentally crossed with another—maybe they culled them or maybe they didn't. Looking around at various strays in different countries, we can see that the mutt is still alive and well.

In places where there are still indigenous populations, you can still see village dogs (a term I've heard mushers use frequently). Village dogs tend to be mutts who hang around the village. In Alaska, for example, some very fast sled dogs have come from village dog lines.

Within the United States, there's been a growing movement to end pet overpopulation. While this is indeed wonderful, it also means you're more likely to see cross-breedings between various purebreds rather than something like a village dog type of mutt. In other words, when you go to an animal shelter, you'll see types or breed mixes: shepherd cross, terrier cross, Beagle mix and so on. We've come full circle with mutts. Mutts begat purebreds and purebreds begat mutts.

GENERAL TYPES OF MIXED BREEDS

So, what should you expect when you look at a particular mixed breed? What characteristics does a particular mix have? Naturally, there are no set rules with a mixed breed and no standardization. However, you may be able to learn about certain behaviors your dog exhibits through the breeds she might have in her.

The Sighthound Type

Dogs mixed with some type of sighthound (Greyhound, Whippet, Pharaoh Hound, Borzoi, etc.) are usually lean and fast. They usually have short coats and may come in white, black, brown, tan or brindle. They have good eyesight (hence the name "sighthound") and can spot animals moving from far off. Their instinct is to pursue movement, and they have what is called a strong prey drive, meaning they will hunt and kill anything they consider food. This includes rabbits, small rodents, cats and herbivores.

Sighthound mixes are normally sweet to people, though some can be independent. Not your best obedience prospects, sighthound mixes usually show some measure of cleverness, but not willingness to obey commands. Some are natural Houdini dogs. Never allow a sighthound mix loose, or you may have trouble recovering her.

Lucky, a Greyhound-shepherd mix, is typical of the sighthound type. He's owned by Mary Elyn Bigos.

*Lightning, an Alaskan Husky with Northern breed
and Greyhound mixed in, owned by the author.*

The Hound (and Sporting) Type

Like sighthounds, hound mixes can be independent. Friendly toward
humans, hounds are usually good with other dogs because their ancestors
often had to hunt in a pack. They tend to be brown, black and tan, red,
white with black or red splotches or ticks, and short-coated. Floppy ears
are common. They are more likely to have a short double coat. Not as
lean and lanky as the sighthound mixes, they are still lean-looking but
may have a thick tail, broad skull and shorter muzzle. Depending on the
type of hound bred in, hound mixes usually are interested in the chase,
but not necessarily the actual kill.

Hounds are usually very independent dogs, but enjoy being with a
pack. They're usually not the best obedience dogs, but they're fun-
loving and they like people. Some can get along with cats if raised with
them; others can't.

Sporting type mixes are a little less like hounds in that they may be
a little more dependent on their owners and more trainable. (Sporting

dogs were trained to follow the hunter's commands and were usually worked one-on-one with their owners).

The Northern Breed Type

The Northern breed mixes will have a double coat and may be gray, white, red, brown, black and tan, black or a variety of those colors. Their ears are usually straight up, but mixes can have floppy ears. Their coats may be short or long or somewhere in between. Their tails will curl over the back. They may have blue, brown or a mixture of blue and brown eyes. They may have huskylike masks.

Northern breed mixes are like sighthounds in that they have excellent eyesight and will pursue prey (they have a high prey drive). Very independent and clever, they can be difficult to train. Many can be Houdini dogs—escape artists.

They like people, but are hard on small animals such as cats, rabbits, birds and rodents. They will hunt if allowed to run loose, so don't let them. Some get along fine with other dogs; other Northern breed mixes are dog aggressive. Northern breeds have plenty of energy and can be extremely destructive if they have no outlet for all that energy.

Chow Chow mixes seem to be prevalent within the Northern breed mixes. I've seen two types of Chow mixes: sweethearts and aloof.

Berkley, a Basenji-Husky mix, owned by Phyllis DeGioia.

Sweetheart Chow mixes are positively the best and most lovable teddy bears. The aloof mixes seem to have inherited their guarding nature from the Chow, and need extra socialization to make them into good pets.

The Shepherd Type

Shepherd mixes usually end up medium to large in size. Most are brown, black and tan, tan or black, but a few may be different colors depending on what was mixed in. Those huge shepherd ears may flop over, depending on the mix. Shepherd mixes are very smart dogs and usually are obedient and very trainable. Most are people-oriented and

A shepherd-Rottweiler mix.

very dependent. Someone told me once that you'll never go to the bathroom alone when you have a shepherd. This is also true with their mixes.

Depending on what is mixed in, shepherd mixes may have a strong guarding instinct. Some are very accepting of strangers but others can be aloof or even aggressive. (Note that good training and socialization can help prevent this.) Many shepherds and shepherd mixes have a fear of loud noises and thunder. Watch for genetic diseases such as hip dysplasia.

The Giant Breed Type
Most giant breed types tend to be a cross of Newfoundland, Saint Bernard, Great Pyrenees, Mastiff or Great Dane. Ears are usually floppy or a combination of upright and dropped. They can be black, red,

Buddy, a Scottie mix.

Sadie, a Pit Bull mix owned by Jessica Faust.

white, brown, black and white, brindle or a mix. They can have short or long coats; most will have double coats.

For the most part, giant breed mixes are gentle dogs, happy to be with you and have fun. Depending on what breed is mixed in, they can be trainable or stubborn. Most are not going to be top obedience dogs. If the dog has Mastiff or other guarding breeds in her, you'll see some tendencies toward protection.

The Terrier Type

The terrier evolved to hunt vermin and small game around farms. It's natural that the terrier personality would be feisty and active. Depending on what terrier your mutt is mixed with, she could be small to medium size. Hair will most likely be coarse and single-coated. Colors could range from white to black to brown to tan and everything in between. Ears can be pricked or dropped. Tails can be long or short.

Terriers are smart and independent. Some do well in obedience, if you can get beyond the independence. Most make good watchdogs. They can be dog aggressive or friendly, depending on the mix. They love to dig.

The Toy and Non-Sporting Types

I've joined these two types together because both toy and non-sporting dogs were generally used as companion animals. These dogs are generally more dependent on their owners. Many are clever and learn tricks easily. They can make good watchdogs. Their size can vary from very small to large, and their coats can either be single or double-coated. They can be any color.

When any of these breed types are mixed, they produce a small to midsize dog with the desire to please her owners. Poodle mixes and Cocker Spaniel mixes tend to be fairly common. These dogs usually have wavy single coats and are highly intelligent.

• •

CHAPTER 3

MIXED RESULTS—FINDING THE PERFECT COMPANION

MIXING IT UP

Now that you know a little about the history of the dog and the role the mutt has played, you may be thinking it's time for you to search for that special canine. But before you start looking, you should decide whether a dog is really in your future. Pet ownership shouldn't be taken lightly. A dog—even a stray or mixed breed—is a 10- to 15-year commitment.

In this chapter, I'll cover the requirements of dog ownership. I'll also discuss your lifestyle and whether a puppy or adult might be best. Finally, I'll discuss where you should you look for your mutt. Should you go to the pound or the local animal shelter? Should you look in the newspaper? You may be surprised at your choices.

SHOULD YOU OWN A DOG?

Are you ready for dog ownership? Dogs require a lot of time—something that many of us do not have. Dogs need food, water, attention and exercise *every day*. They need training—even adult dogs. Do you have the time it takes to train your dog? Consider the following questions when you're getting ready to adopt or purchase a dog or puppy:

- A dog is a 10- to 15-year commitment. Are you willing to rearrange your life for 10 to 15 years to care for a dog?
- Can you be home every day or make arrangements so that your dog can eat, drink, exercise and relieve himself?

- Will *you* take care of your dog? Children can't take responsibility for a dog—no matter what they say. A dog must be the responsibility of an adult in the household.

- Are you willing to put up with a certain amount of destructiveness associated with a dog? Puppies have accidents, and even adult dogs do from time to time. Puppies and adult dogs may chew inappropriate items.

- Are you willing to housetrain (housebreak) your dog?

- Are you willing to groom your dog as required? Some breeds and mixes require more grooming than others, but all dogs need a good brushing at least once a week. Dogs with double coats will shed profusely, and some breeds require clipping. All dogs must have their nails clipped regularly.

- Can you spend time training your dog so he is enjoyable and fun to be around?

- Can you leave a puppy alone for no more than four hours and leave an adult dog alone for no longer than nine hours?

- Do you have a fenced-in backyard that is dig-proof, climb-proof and jump-proof? If you do not, can you walk your dog on a leash several times a day to let him relieve himself?

- Are you willing to pick up after your dog? Many cities have ordinances requiring that dog owners clean up after their dog defecates.

- Are you willing to put up with dog hair, dirty clothes (from being jumped on) and other messes that go with having a dog?

- Is anyone in your family allergic to dogs? If anyone is, a dog may not be a good choice for your family.

- Does everyone in your family want a dog? Everyone must agree on wanting a dog.

- Are you willing to exercise your dog every day? Activity levels of dogs differ considerably, but all dogs need daily exercise.

- Can you afford a dog? A free or lowcost dog is *not* a free dog. You must buy dog food, bowls, dog beds, dog toys and grooming items. You must pay for routine veterinary care and other care should the medical need arise.

If you've answered yes to all these questions, you're ready to consider owning a dog.

Should you own a dog? Dogs require time and attention. This is Boo, a Beagle-shepherd mix, and Lucky, a Greyhound-shepherd mix, owned by Mary Elyn Bigos.

FINDING YOUR TYPE

Once you've determined you'll make a good dog owner, your next step is to decide what type of dog you're looking for. Not all dogs are the same—just as not all people are the same. Dogs come in various shapes and sizes—and personalities. You can learn more about your potential dog's personality by learning about the breeds in his background (see Chapter 2).

You need to decide what size of dog is important to you. You need to decide whether you want a puppy or an adult, a male or a female. And you need to determine what personality will be compatible with you and your lifestyle. Your choice should be a matter of personal preference—there are no wrong answers here unless the dog doesn't suit you.

Large, Medium or Small?

Size does matter—especially with dogs. You probably already have a preference. But before you decide on a particular size, consider the following:

- Small and medium dogs are good for apartment dwellers or people with limited strength or lower activity levels. They're also good for people with small yards.
- Medium and large dogs can be intimidating to strangers but may make a person living alone feel more secure.
- Medium and large dogs generally need fenced-in yards and more exercise than smaller breeds.
- Large dogs are good for people who live athletic lifestyles or need athletic dogs.
- Medium dogs often offer a compromise between large and small dogs.

Not all dogs are the same in personality.
This is Berkley, a Basenji-Husky mix, and
Fred, a Westie-Bichon mix, owned by Phyllis DeGioia.

There are caveats that go with these rules. For example, many terriers and terrier-mixes can be very active even though they're small (Jack Russell Terriers and their mixes, for example) and would not necessarily be suited to an owner who wants a dog with a low activity level. Some large dogs, such as retired Greyhounds, can live in an apartment because of their couch potato temperaments.

Puppy or Adult?

Certainly, there's nothing more adorable than a puppy. One look into a puppy's soulful eyes and you're gone. Who, except those with the strongest will, can resist a puppy?

There's something to be said for a puppy. If you get a puppy younger than four months, it is like starting with a clean slate. The puppy hasn't had time to learn bad habits. You also get the joy of see-ing your puppy grow into an adult dog.

But before you rush out and pick your ball of fluffy fur, sit back and think a moment. Do you have the time to take care of a puppy? Puppies don't come housebroken, and many take months to housebreak. They don't know the rules and will chew inappropriate items. They require more attention than an adult dog and need more socialization, training and exercise. If no one is around during the day, you might wish to reconsider your desire to own a puppy.

Because you're considering a mixed breed, you may be in for a sur-prise as your puppy grows. ("Wow! I didn't know he would be this big.")

Adult and adolescent dogs are usually housebroken (or can be housebroken easily) and may know some obedience commands. An adult dog will have settled down a bit and won't need all the attention and exercise a puppy requires. There aren't too many surprises with an adult dog—what you see is what you get. However, an adult dog may have picked up bad habits from previous owners or may have been traumatized during his life. In this case, training and socialization are important for these dogs.

Adult dogs generally aren't as easily adoptable as puppies. If you're looking to rescue a dog from a shelter, the most needy ones are adult dogs.

Male or Female?

The next choice is male or female. For the most part, this is a personal preference, because both males and females make excellent pets. If you're a first-time dog owner, a female may be a better choice because they are less likely to challenge you.

*Don't discount the adult. An adult dog has settled down a bit—
enough to put up with a hat! Zoe is owned by Maggie Meleski.*

In some breeds, females tend to be more dependent and males more
independent. In other breeds, the reverse is true. With mixed breeds,
you can't make these assumptions, so be ready to rely on personality
tests to determine which puppy or dog is right for you.

Since you are getting a mixed breed, you should be spaying or
neutering him. Spaying—that is, removing the female's reproductive
organs—generally costs more than neutering and is a major surgery
when compared to neutering. However, a good veterinarian who
has performed spays routinely should not have any problems spaying
your dog.

Personality Plus

So how do you decide which dog is right for you? Quite often,
we decide on the basis of looks. But a good-looking dog with a temperament that doesn't suit you is a recipe for disaster. Not all dog

personalities are the same, just as not all people are the same. However, there are tendencies in each breed.

Your lifestyle and personality will greatly affect whether you and your new canine companion are compatible. Some mixed breeds have breeds in them that are independent; others have breeds in them that are trainable and want to please.

Decide what you're willing to accept and what is unacceptable. For example, some people want a very trainable dog who loves to obey every command. Others like a dog who's an independent thinker. Think about what activities you're planning on doing with your dog. Maybe you're happy with a house pet—that's great! But if you're planning on doing activities with your dog, such as backpacking, agility or flyball, you may want a different personality than a couch potato.

Breed Characteristics

The purebreds that we know of came about because people needed a dog to do a job. Whether it was pulling a sled, herding sheep or being a lap warmer, dogs filled the niche admirably. Some dogs were better at certain jobs than others. People bred these dogs to other dogs who showed the same traits, and thus, purebreds appeared.

Ironically, most mixed breeds are now mixes of purebred dogs. These mixed breeds have the traits of their ancestors. A dog who has Australian Cattle Dog in him is likely to show herding and guarding instincts. A dog who is a Husky mix is likely to be independent and like to pull. A terrier mix will enjoy digging. Understanding the heritage of your dog is crucial to harmony.

KIDS AND DOGS

If you have children, you need to consider them before getting a dog. Every year, children are bit—some seriously—because their parents left them alone with a dog. Many children do not understand the difference between a dog and a stuffed toy. Dogs aren't playthings, and even the gentlest dog may bite if he's in pain or provoked. If you have very young children, you must teach them that dogs are not toys and can feel pain. Even so, you should never leave a young child unsupervised with a dog at any time.

Older children can help you care for the dog, but the care should always be under adult supervision.

TWO'S COMPANY

If you already have another dog, you should look for a dog who will be compatible with your current dog. Your new dog should be roughly the same size as your current dog when fully grown. Choosing a dog of the opposite sex to your current dog may also reduce potential spats, as will having both dogs neutered or spayed. If your current dog shows aggression toward other dogs, you should reconsider getting a second dog.

NO CHRISTMAS PUPPIES, PLEASE!

You may think that getting a dog or puppy around the holidays (Christmas, Hanukkah, Easter, etc.) is a perfect time. Or perhaps giving a dog or puppy to a loved one might be the perfect gift. Nothing could be further from the truth.

The holidays are a time for family and friends to get together. Most families are too busy at this time to properly care for a new puppy or dog. If you're planning to adopt a dog as a Christmas present to your family, give family members dog toys and supplies as part of their presents, to use when you go *after* the holidays to find your perfect pet.

Likewise, never give a puppy or dog to someone as a present. If you know the person wants a new dog, give them dog supplies and then offer to go with them to help them adopt a new pet. That way, they can select the perfect pet for them.

WHERE TO FIND YOUR MUTT

Now that you've decided you're ready for your new companion, you may be wondering where is the best place to find a mixed breed. There are an overwhelming number of places to find a mixed breed dog—from shelters and rescue groups to off the street to your neighbor's backyard. What place is really the best?

The truth is that any place that has unwanted pets is a good place to adopt your dog. It may be the neighbor next door whose dog had puppies or it may be the local shelter. It may be the stray you find wandering in the park, who was dumped by an owner who no longer loved him.

Shelters or Rescue

Naturally, the first place you may think of when looking for a mutt is the local pound, animal shelter or rescue group. Three-quarters of all dogs brought to the shelter are mixed breeds. That includes crosses such as Labrador Retriever and Australian Shepherd mixes and dogs who aren't any discernable mix of breeds. Indeed, some shelters may actually call certain dogs "mixes" even though they are purebred, because they do not have any actual papers proving their pedigrees. The reverse might also be true.

If you've picked up this book with the intention of finding the right mutt for you, you probably don't care if your dog has registration papers or not. In this case, whether your dog is purebred or not shouldn't make a difference.

There are two types of shelters—no-kill and kill shelters. The no-kill shelters do not put to death any animals brought to them, but because of this, they frequently turn down pets while trying to find homes for their current dogs. Depending on their policies, they may or may not have what are considered "unadoptable animals," that is, dogs who are too old or have a serious medical or behavioral problem that would prevent them from being adopted.

Kill shelters, as the term implies, put pets to death if they are not adopted after a certain amount of time. Depending on how busy a shelter is, it could mean anywhere from a day to a few weeks.

This dog, at my local shelter, is just waiting for someone to take him home.

Rescue is another place to look for dogs. Most rescue dogs are purebred, but some groups rescue mixed breeds as well. A rescue group is not necessarily a place, like a shelter, but may actually be several volunteers who foster dogs in their homes. Volunteers working with organizations such as a national breed club typically run rescue groups. They are usually understaffed and overworked and need money and more volunteers.

Adoption procedures vary greatly in many shelters and rescues. Most shelters and rescue groups require that you spay or neuter the dog, or will do that for you before you bring the dog home. Most screen applicants to avoid having the dog returned to them or putting the dog in a situation that would be worse than his current one.

What age range can you find at shelters and rescues? Usually all age ranges, but most dogs are between six months and five years old. Generally, puppies and kittens are most popular, followed by young adolescent animals, adults and finally, the older pets. Purebreds tend to be a bit more popular than mutts, so if you're looking simply to give a dog a second chance, dogs with the lowest chance of placement are older, mixed breed dogs.

Shelters and rescue groups usually offer adoptable animals—that is, dogs who appear to be healthy and well-adjusted. Dogs who are sick with an incurable disease, are aggressive or have other problems are usually euthanized. However, don't assume this is the case. If you look at a dog in a shelter or rescue, ask what his background is. Why was he turned in? What is his history? Sometimes, but not always, the shelter or rescue can tell you about the dog. If the dog was turned in for aggression or serious health problems, you should probably reconsider your choice.

Hard Luck Cases

This brings up the topic of hard luck cases. There are plenty of them out there—but should you consider a hard luck case? Typical hard luck cases include:

- Senior dogs—dogs over eight years old
- Dogs who are severely ill or have a terminal condition
- Dogs who have personality disorders or ones who require psychopharmaceuticals such as Prozac to maintain a good temperament

- Dogs who have an extremely expensive medical condition such as hip dysplasia
- Dogs who have bitten people

If you're a dog professional or someone who has had many dogs and enjoys the challenge of a rescue, perhaps my next statements will not apply to you. With the exception of senior dogs, if this is your first dog or if you're looking for a companion, run—don't walk—away from hard luck cases. Most hard luck cases aren't worth the time or effort when there are so many healthier, well-adjusted dogs waiting to be taken home. Indeed, many hard luck cases should be euthanized. It is humane to euthanize aggressive dogs who are a liability, sick dogs who can't be cured and are in pain and dogs with terminal diseases. You, the dog owner, should not have to pay for a sick animal or shoulder the responsibility for someone else's problems.

My caveat in the hard luck cases is senior dogs. Senior dogs make excellent pets. Most are housebroken and know some obedience commands. Gone are the wild puppy days—they're more content to sit beside you and enjoy your companionship. They appreciate a warm fire and a soft bed. And they enjoy having someone to share their last years with.

The truth is that we tend to call dogs "senior" when they are over seven years old, but in reality, those dogs are often in the prime of their life. I've had dogs live past 16 years old, and all have lived a good life. With proper nutrition, exercise, veterinary care and good genetics, there's no reason a six- or seven-year-old dog can't live five to 10 more years. Toy dogs, for example, usually live past 15 years. Even large dogs can live extraordinarily long.

Streetwise Dogs

Occasionally, people become dog owners by picking up a stray. Strays are definitely a risky proposition, but I've done it with success and others have, too. In many instances, strays are dumped dogs; that is, the owner was too afraid to take the dog to a shelter and instead decided to give the dog "the long car ride." Sadly, these people dump the dogs off in the country or wilderness areas or by the side of a highway, thinking someone will take them in or the dogs will manage to fend for themselves. The truth is, this is like dumping a five-year-old child in the

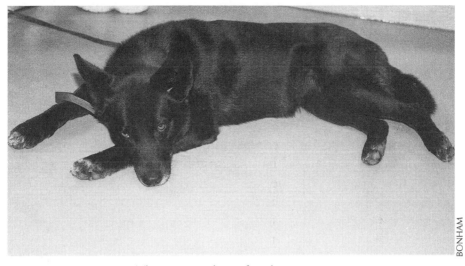

This pretty girl was found as a stray.

middle of nowhere and telling him to fend for himself. The prospect for survival is grim, at best.

But not all strays are abandoned dogs. Indeed, some are lost dogs looking for their owner. Others are dogs whose owners have the mistaken notion that dogs should run loose. This is why when you find a stray, you should make a reasonable attempt to find the owner. Many papers offer free "found dog" ads for people who attempt to locate a dog's owners.

When you find a stray, the first thing you should do is check for any identification. Collar and tags, tattoos and microchips are all possible forms of identification. Tattoos are located on the inside of the thigh or in the ears. (You may have to part the fur to find it.) If you find a tattoo, you should contract National Dog Registry, Tattoo-A-Pet, Companion Animal Recovery and any other national registry to have them search their databases for the dog's ID. Microchips, however, can only be read with a scanner. Veterinarians and shelters may have scanners to check for chips, but not all scanners can read all chips. Once you figure out what type of chip, you must contact the registry for information regarding the dog.

Strays may have a multitude of health problems. Many have worms, fleas, mange or other parasites and may be starving. Strays often mistrust humans because of the injustice done to them. They may have been shot at or had things thrown at them. They may be fearful and cringing. The health problems, such as parasites and malnutrition, can be corrected. The emotional trauma may take some time to heal—if it ever does. But strays can become happy members of your family with patience and love. I have taken in two strays with great success—one had suffered abuse—which shows how resilient dogs actually are.

Newshounds

Sometimes you can find the perfect pet looking in the newspaper classifieds. Often, these dogs are offered "free to a good home" or for a nominal fee. You can find puppies and adults through the paper.

If you decide to look for your next dog in the newspaper, you should ask why the owner is selling or giving away the dog. There are various reasons that owners give away their pets. The generic reason—often given because the owner doesn't want to go into lengthy explanations—is allergies. While there are dogs whose owners suddenly become allergic, many can tolerate their pets if they take allergy medication. In fact, one study suggests children with allergies who grow up in pet homes are actually more resistant to allergens.

Often, people purchase puppies without understanding the true commitment required. These pups grow into adolescent terrors without proper discipline. While a dog who has bad habits can be trained (indeed, many owners give up their dogs because of bad habits), you should find out if the dog is aggressive.

You can find out easily if the dog is being given up because of bad habits. Ask the owner what commands the dog knows and if he is housetrained. No training or minimal training is indicative of a dog who needs training and possibly needs to be cured of his bad habits. Where the dog sleeps is also a good indication of how the dog fits into the family. If the dog sleeps outside, in the garage or in the basement, the family has very little attachment to the dog.

Other reasons for giving away or selling a dog include:

- Change of lifestyle or income
- Owner died
- Moving
- Family pet had puppies

Uh-oh! She Was Pregnant?

Amazingly, many owners of intact female dogs are surprised when their female has puppies. Despite campaigns for spay and neuter, the owner doesn't spay their female dog and she gets out just once while she's in season. Sixty-three days later—puppies!

Purebred owners tend to keep their females intact because they mistakenly think their female is somehow more valuable because she is purebred. One litter of puppies usually convinces most owners to get their female dog spayed, but they've already added to the pet overpopulation problem. While there are still many mutt puppies, most "accidents" are the product of accidental crossbreeding.

The downside to puppies from accidents is quite often that the father is unknown and the parents were never screened for genetic diseases such as hip dysplasia or eye diseases. If you choose a puppy from an accidental breeding, you are taking a risk on the puppy being genetically unhealthy. However, this is a problem with all mixed breeds, since most have never been screened for genetic health problems. (More on genetic diseases and choosing a dog in Chapter 4.)

Bruiser, a "Cockapoo," owned by Phyllis DeGioia. Cockapoos are not rare, nor are they breeds.

A Note on "Breeders"

Breeders of crossbreed dogs—Peekapoos, Cockapoos and the like—are breeding mixed breed dogs. These dogs are not registered and are no more valuable than any other mutt. No legitimate registry recognizes these crossbreds, who often go for hundreds of dollars.

Avoid these breeders at all costs! Not only are they producing mixed breeds at a purebred price, but it is highly unlikely that these dogs are screened for genetic diseases.

CHAPTER 4

ALL MIXED UP—FINDING THE RIGHT MUTT

You've decided that a mutt is the right dog for you. But how do you find the perfect mixed breed? Mutts come in all shapes and sizes, all colors and, most important, all personalities. They can be the quintessential mush-pot who would love nothing more than to be a couch potato the rest of their lives, or they can be very active and will play for hours on end or even pull a sled. Your lifestyle should dictate what kind of dog you want.

LOOKING FOR MR. (OR MS.) RIGHT

So, what are you looking for in a dog? If you're like most people, you probably haven't given it much thought. Give some thought to it now. Are you looking for a dog primarily as a companion? Someone to go with you on walks and lie down beside you while you watch those old movies on Saturday afternoons? Or are you looking for the next flyball or agility champion? Maybe you'd enjoy having a dog jogging beside you while you ride your bike five miles every day. Or maybe you want a dog who sounds big but greets your friends with a happy lick when they stop by for a visit.

If you've already decided that your lifestyle would be more suited to an adult dog, your next step is to determine how much of an adult you want. How active, how independent do you want your dog to be? Dogs vary considerably in independence. Some owners hate independent dogs because the dogs don't appear to care much about whether or not they please their owners. On the exact opposite side are owners who hate clingy dogs. Some owners want dogs who like everyone they meet, while other owners like dogs who are "one person" or "one family" dogs.

Looking for a couch potato? There are mixed breeds who are happy to comply. This is Sadie, a Pit Bull mix owned by Jessica Faust.

Looking for an agility or flyball champion? Mixed breeds can fit the bill. This is Robyn, a Golden-Cocker mix owned by Kathy and Jim Stabler.

The good news is that because the mutt personality is so varied, you can find a unique dog who will fit your personality. The following list of statements is designed to help you decide the kind of dog you're looking for—one who will fit with your personality and with your lifestyle. Look at each statement and decide whether it applies to you. Answer honestly—there are no right or wrong answers. The phrases in parentheses indicate what kind of dog would be compatible with a person who agrees with the statement.

1. I am physically active in outdoor sports three times a week or more and would enjoy doing such activities with a dog. (High activity)

2. I like to stay home and enjoy quiet time. I would like a dog who would also enjoy that. (Low activity, non-dominant)

3. I hike, camp, backpack or hunt for recreation and would enjoy bringing along a dog. (High activity)

4. I like a dog who is with me most of the time. (High dependence, non-dominant)

5. I like a dog who is independent and doesn't need to be by my side constantly. (Low dependence)

6. I must have a dog who obeys my commands consistently. I want a dog I can easily train. (High to medium dependence, high trainability, non-dominant)

7. I don't want a dog who is hyper. (Low to medium activity)

8. I have children. (Non dominant)

9. I have another dog or cat. (Non-dominant)

10. I would like a dog who will be a natural watchdog. (High to medium activity, medium dependence)

11. I want a dog who doesn't shed. (Single coat dogs)

12. I don't want a very active dog. (Low to medium activity)

13. I have a disability or I am not very strong. (Small to medium size, low to medium activity, high trainability, non-dominant)

14. I am looking for a house pet I can enjoy, but not necessarily a canine athlete. (Low to medium activity, non-dominant)

15. I want a low-maintenance dog when it comes to grooming. (Short hair)

When you're looking for a dog, you must consider your situation. Do you have young children? Are you elderly or do you have a disability? Are you physically active and looking for a dog who will share that lifestyle? Are you looking for a pet? Do you hate the idea of brushing and combing a dog every day? All these factors need to be considered when you look for your dog. What is the ideal dog for one person isn't the right dog for someone else.

When you're thinking about a dog, go beyond her good looks. What's her personality like? You need a dog who will fit in with your life. Some dogs, like those mixes from Northern breeds, can be very independent-minded and may not make good watchdogs, but will enjoy going hiking with you. Terriers can be independent and active. Poodle mixes can be very person-oriented, but may need clipping if they have single coats. Sighthound mixes may have soft temperaments but may chase after a cat or a piece of paper blowing in the wind.

When you consider a mix, consider the following generalities:

- Shepherd mixes are usually highly trainable, have medium to high activity levels, and may have a fair amount of dependence.
- Northern breed mixes are not as easily trained, have a medium to high activity level, and are usually independent. Many are dominant.
- Hound mixes are not as easily trained, have a low to high activity level, and are usually independent.
- Sporting dog mixes are usually highly trainable, have medium to high activity levels, and may have a fair amount of dependence.
- Toy dog mixes are usually highly trainable, have low to high activity levels, and may have a fair amount of dependence.
- Non-sporting dog mixes are usually trainable, have low to medium activity levels, and may have some dependence.
- Terriers are trainable to not as easily trained, have medium to high activity levels, and are usually independent.

Note that these are generalities and that there will be differences, depending on the types of breeds in the mix.

Once you've determined the type of personality you're looking for, along with certain physical characteristics, you're ready to look for your puppy or adult dog. Be aware that the activity level of a puppy is much higher than that of an adult.

SELECTING YOUR PUPPY

Depending on where you go to find your puppy, you may or may not have much background to go on. If you visit someone whose dog has had an accidental litter, you'll know the mother's breed but you may not know the father's breed, unless the owners have the dog or unless the owner is sure which neighbor's dog bred her. In many cases, it's a matter of guessing.

No matter how adorable those puppies are, do not take a puppy away from her mother before she is eight weeks old. (In some states, it is against the law.) A puppy needs to spend time with her mother and siblings for socialization and to develop her own personality. If you take a puppy away from her mother much earlier, you run the risk of personality problems that will plague that dog throughout her entire life.

First, consider the health of the puppies. Are they bright-eyed, eager and alert? Are they clean and is their coat shiny? They shouldn't be too fat or thin, nor should they have a potbelly—indicative of worms. They might be sleepy if they just woke from a nap, but they shouldn't be sluggish or unresponsive. Avoid puppies who cry or act unhappy—there's usually an underlying problem with them.

When you visit a litter of puppies, kneel down and clap your hands. Some puppies may seem interested in you; others may ignore you. The ones who ignore you are usually the independent ones. The puppy who comes over first may be an alpha, that is, a dominant personality. While alpha puppies are great for those who are used to that personality, if you've never had an alpha dog, consider taking a puppy who is less dominant. Alphas will tend to rule the roost and will challenge you at every opportunity.

Most alpha puppies will not accept being gently put on their back and held there, while most non-dominant puppies will accept it after a slight fuss. An overly submissive dog will lie on her back without a struggle. But a very submissive dog is as poor a choice as a very dominant dog.

Determining trainability is difficult at this age. You will have to rely on knowing what breeds are in the puppy's background to decide how trainable the puppy will be. Certainly, intelligence plays a role in a puppy's trainability, but not all smart dogs are highly trainable. Indeed, some very intelligent dogs have an independent streak—they know what you want, but they just don't feel it is in their best interest to do what you want.

Likewise, it's difficult to tell what kind of coat the puppy will have or how big she will grow. You can make an educated guess if you know what at least one of her parents looked like or know what breeds they were. If the puppy is a crossbreed of a larger dog and a smaller dog, you can guess she will be somewhere in between the two. If the puppy is truly a mix, not just a crossbreed, you may be in for a surprise. You can judge somewhat by her size at eight weeks, but she may still surprise you.

Pick out your prospective puppy and separate her from her littermates. She should be a little apprehensive at first, but then with petting and encouragement, she should accept you cheerfully. If she cringes or acts submissive, or becomes aggressive or hyper, consider another puppy.

If there are toys available, roll a ball in front of the puppy. She should chase it or at least watch it as it rolls. Look at her eyes for cloudiness or murkiness, which may indicate juvenile cataracts. Clap your hands behind her head to see if she reacts to the sound. You will want a puppy who can at least hear and see. Some breeds, such as Dalmatians and Australian Shepherds, have congenital deafness in their lines, which can show up in mixed breeds as well.

SELECTING AN ADULT DOG

Selecting an adult or adolescent dog is a little less of a mystery. If the dog is an adult, what you see is what you get. There are no size surprises and the coat on the dog is generally the type of coat she will always have. Her personality is set too—if she's a non-dominant sweetie, she's likely to stay that way unless there's an underlying health problem. Adult dogs are usually housebroken, or can be housebroken more easily than puppies. She may know a few commands and may even have learned a few tricks.

Adolescent dogs are generally big puppies who have hit the obnoxious phase of their life. Like human adolescents, they can be a challenging handful or they can be sweet-tempered. The obnoxious behavior may have begun. If they have a rebellious streak in them, they're attitude is "make me." They usually have a case of the "uglies"— they're gangly and clumsy now. Their hair sticks out in all directions. They're all feet and ears. They'll turn into a handsome adult someday, but the puppy cuteness has worn off. They're also a lot of fun.

Find out all you can about an adult dog before you meet with her. Why did the owner give up this dog? Remember that the word "allergies" is often a way for people to avoid talking about the real issue, which may be behavioral. Don't be confrontational, but sometimes when you ask about what training the dog has, the owner may admit to certain behavioral problems. ("She isn't housebroken." "She barks all night when we leave her outside.")

When you're adopting from a shelter, you may have little to go on. But if you talk to the shelter workers there, they may have some information about the dog. ("Her owners were moving." "She's very sweet, but pulls on a leash when you walk her.") They may also have some health information.

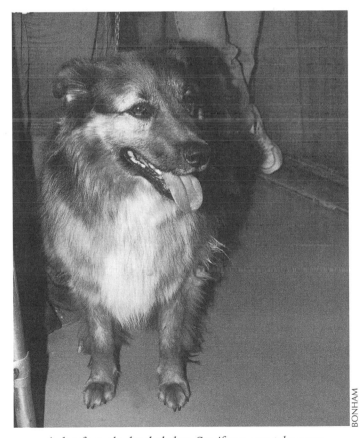

*A dog from the local shelter. See if you can take your
prospective dog someplace where you can interact
with her separately, away from all the other dogs.*

When you meet the dog, see if you can take her someplace where you can meet her separately. (Most shelters have meeting rooms for prospective owners.) When you meet with an adult dog in a shelter, remember that the shelter is a very stressful place for dogs and you may not see the dog's true personality there. Still, if the dog does well in this environment, you can often assume she would do even better in a calmer environment.

Personality tests are harder with adult dogs. Unlike puppies, adult dogs may take serious exception to being rolled over. (Most adult dogs consider this an aggressive behavior and you are most likely to get bit while trying it.) Instead, approach an adult dog in a gentle and non-threatening manner. When you meet the dog, kneel down to greet her. Watch her behavior toward you—is she happy to meet you or cringing and fearful? If she is happy and friendly, you can introduce yourself. If the dog is cringing and fearful, don't push! This could result in a quick fear bite.

Avoid any dog who is aggressive or fearful. Remember, there are plenty of well-adjusted dogs in need of good homes. Don't try to force any dog to accept your petting or your touch. Look for another dog.

If the mutt you're considering is friendly, offer your hand to sniff. Be calm and relaxed, not stiff, when offering your hand. Rigidity is a sure sign of challenge to a dog, and many will become fearful or aggressive if you tense up. Likewise, don't try to pet the dog on top of the head—this is very dominant. Instead, the dog may accept an underhand chin tickle. Once you're on good terms with the dog, you can try taking her for a walk and perhaps see if she knows any commands.

If the dog knows commands, walk her on a leash and practice the commands. Don't be surprised if she pulls on a leash—this is very common when a dog is excited. Offer her a dog biscuit whenever she performs a command correctly.

Call the dog to you and clap your hands. She should show interest at the sound of a friendly voice, but she may also show some independence and may not come immediately, or may not come at all without food to lure her. Watch for any unusual behavior. If the dog seems odd or does very unexpected things, look elsewhere.

Look at the overall health of the dog. Are her eyes clear and bright? Is her coat healthy? If she's been in the shelter for some time, her coat may not be as clean as you might like. She should look healthy and be free from serious health problems. If she will let you examine her, do so gently. Look at her ears and teeth if she will let you. Her ears should be clean and her gums should be free of redness and swelling. She should walk without a limp. Many shelters will give you a health guarantee, but you must have a veterinarian examine your mutt within a certain amount of time. If you are adopting your mutt from a private party, ask for a written guarantee stating that the owner will take back the dog if a veterinarian finds her to be unhealthy within 72 hours. Then take the dog to the veterinarian.

SELECTING A SENIOR DOG

Selecting a senior dog is much like selecting an adult dog, with one exception: Some health problems are to be expected. Senior dogs are more prone to arthritis, bad teeth and cancers. Medications can mitigate arthritis, a trip to the doggie dentist can usually fix teeth problems and many tumors are operable, but it's up to you to determine how much you're willing to do to own an older dog.

Remember that not all "older dogs" are that old. In many cases, dogs can live from 10 to 15 years or more, which makes dogs of seven years merely middle-aged. Many are still in the prime of their lives.

IS SHE GOOD WITH KIDS?

Not all dogs are good with kids. If you have children, you should definitely find a dog who likes children. When you've narrowed down your selection, bring the family to meet the potential new addition. Put the dog in a waiting room, then bring in one family member. After the dog has met one family member, have that person leave and another one come in. Observe your potential dog's reaction to each person. Excitement is expected, but growling or snapping is not.

LEARNING YOUR MUTT'S HISTORY

If you can, ask the owner or shelter about this dog's past. Why was she turned in? Does she know any commands? Is she housebroken? Why did the owners give her up? Questions like these may shed more light on your dog's past and enable you to make an informed decision about whether this is the right dog for you.

If the shelter workers are talkative, find out how the dog does in the shelter. But remember, a shelter is a scary place for a dog—there's a lot of barking and crying here. There are many strange smells—not all of them pleasant. What's more, the dog sees an extraordinary number of people every day—but not one she can feel secure about or bond with. With this type of environment, it's a wonder that all shelter dogs aren't nervous wrecks.

WHAT IS SHE?

What in the world could she be? Mixed breeds can offer a strange combination of characteristics you might never expect: up ears, down ears, ears that lie on the sides; short, squat noses or long noses; long and thin or short and stocky. And what do you call that color? Brown, brindle, sable, red, white, spotted, blue merle?

My first dog, Conan, was a Newfoundland-Samoyed cross. He was the only black puppy in his litter and had webbed feet—like a Newfoundland. His siblings had white coats but one of his brothers had a black and white coat. His sister, who later had an accidental litter (owned by someone else), was bred by a Golden Retriever. The subsequent puppies were light golden and looked nothing like the Samoyed and Newfoundland in their background.

Another dog I owned, Mirin, was obviously a Husky cross with blue eyes and prick ears, but she looked more like a white Basenji. Who knows what gave her the short coat and the terrier head?

When you look at your dog, realize that what you're doing is making an educated guess. If the dog's ancestry is unknown, your guess is no worse that the guesses the shelter workers make.

German Shepherd Mixes

German Shepherd mixes are fairly common. Usually the dogs are medium to large and may have a short or long coat. They may be black and tan or solid black. Usually they have a head that looks similar to a German Shepherd, with brown or even golden eyes. As puppies, they have enormous ears and feet and tend to be mouthy. They're very dependent on their humans and love to follow you around. Their bodies can be blocky, but if they have the true shepherd body, they tend to have oval rather than barrel chests.

Retriever Mixes

These dogs tend to be blocky and square, with floppy ears and thick tails. Depending on what they're mixed with, they may look very much

What is she? Sometimes you can get an idea of what your dog might have in her, and sometimes you can't. This is Chelsea, owned by Natalie Rowe, who may or may not be part Labrador Retriever, part shepherd and who knows what else.

like their retriever ancestor, but with some changes to the coat or ear carriage. The mix will affect their muzzle and head, but you should see a retriever look about them. Common colors are black and yellow, but chocolate can appear as well.

Husky Mixes

Blue eyes are usually a giveaway for a Husky mix, but not always. Some breeds, such as Dalmatians, Australian Shepherds, and Australian Cattle Dogs, may also have blue eyes. Huskies may have blue eyes, brown eyes, golden eyes or even bi-eyes (one blue and one brown). Husky mixes have thick, double coats, regardless of whether they are short or long. They may be as small as 30 pounds or heavier than 75 pounds, depending on what's mixed with them. They can be any color, but will have the characteristic tail that curls over the top of the back.

Chow Mixes

Like Husky mixes, Chow mixes usually have tails that curl over the top of their back. However, unlike Husky mixes, Chow mixes are usually blocky and square in their body and usually have a blue-black or partially blue tongue. Their muzzle might be short or long, depending on the breed mixed with them. They usually come in black, red or fawn, but you may see other colors as well. They may have prick or floppy ears.

Sighthound Mixes

Long and lean, sighthound mixes may have the body of a Greyhound. They may have long or short hair, depending on the mix. They can come in all colors, but some of the most striking sighthounds have brindling (black and brown stripes).

Poodle Mixes

Poodle mixes are fairly common, especially when you consider that there are breeders producing "Cockapoos" (Cocker Spaniel and Poodle crosses) and "Peekapoos" (Pekingese and Poodle crosses). If a dog has a single coat, that is, a coat without an undercoat, the dog may have Poodle in her. Her coat may be curly or wavy, but never harsh (a hard, harsh coat suggests a terrier mix). Floppy ears and a small to medium body may also be indicative of a Poodle, although there are certainly crosses between larger Standard Poodles.

Terrier Mixes

Terriers are quite popular. Any dog with a single coat that feels wiry or bristly may have terrier in her. Terriers are anywhere from very small (Jack Russell Terrier) to large (Airedale), but you can probably expect a mix to be a small to medium size dog. She may have prick or floppy ears. The most notable thing about a terrier mix is her spirit and the intelligence in her eyes. If she looks like an imp ready to get into trouble, you can bet there's some terrier in her.

Hound Mixes

Hounds have solid bodies with floppy ears. They usually have a short coat, and, depending on what they're mixed with, may have some unusual colors. You can recognize a hound mix by her deep, throaty bay. She will most likely have looser skin and a heavier bone structure, as well, not to mention a tail that will sweep anything off the table.

Herding Breed Mixes

Herding breed mixes tend to be medium size and may have a short or long coat. They can be any color, but if they follow their herding breed's color, they may be blue merle, red merle, tricolor, black and white or sable. Usually they have a strong stop (the indent where the skull meets the muzzle), prick or floppy ears, and a very intelligent expression. Those with Australian Shepherd or Border Collie in their ancestry may stare intently at you. They may also try to nip at your heels as you walk.

Wolf Hybrids

Wolf hybrids are difficult to detect. Most dogs purported to be wolf mixes are usually Malamute, Husky or even shepherd mixes. Some so-called experts have mislabeled many dogs as being hybrids when they are not. Wolf hybrids are illegal in many municipalities, and many shelters will put down a known hybrid.

The problem is that there is no single test for hybrids, nor are there any particular characteristics that one can point to and say, "That comes from a wolf." For example, many wolves and wolf hybrids have golden or "brass" eyes. However, purebred Huskies and Malamutes can have those same color eyes. The agouti color, reminiscent of a wolf, can be found in Alaskan Malamutes, Siberian Huskies and Alaskan Huskies. Wolf hybrids can also be white or black. Wolves tend to be rangy and have large paws, but anyone who has owned a German Shepherd Dog/Malamute cross can attest to their dog's ranginess. Wolves heads tend to have almond-shaped eyes and less of a stop, but Malamutes and Huskies may have similar heads.

Possibly the most reliable indication of a wolf hybrid might be the aloof personality, but again, I've seen Huskies with not an ounce of wolf in them (except maybe 5,000 years ago) be aloof and I've seen wolf hybrids who would lick your face. The best indication is to see how the dogs reacts to people and other dogs. Most hybrids are aloof with people and act wolfy with other dogs. High-percentage wolf hybrids have a wildness in them that makes them unpredictable. Low percentage hybrids may act more dog than wolf, but it depends a lot on the genetics.

Never adopt a known wolf hybrid unless you are very experienced with handling wolves. A hybrid is a mix of domesticated dog and wild animal. The random gene mixture may create a dog with a stable temperament, but it's doubtful. Most of the time, the resulting dog is unpredictable and unsafe. In some cases, hybrids have triggers that may cause them to bite after months of model behavior.

WHEN A PUREBRED LOOKS LIKE A MUTT

Occasionally you may find a dog you think is a mutt who is a purebred of an unusual or rare breed. How can you tell if your dog is a rare breed or even an unusual breed?

I have good news and bad news. The bad news is that there isn't a purebred test to tell you your dog is a rare breed and not a mutt. The good news is that there are plenty of breed books with pictures of various dog breeds, including rare breeds. If you look at some pictures and suspect your dog might be a rare breed, contact the rare breed club (usually registered through UKC) and then contact breeders to get their assessment of your dog.

Whether your dog is a purebred or a mutt won't make a difference as to whether she'll make a fine pet.

PUREBREDS WHO LOOK LIKE THEY COULD BE MUTTS

- Chinook
- Carolina Dog
- Canaan Dog
- Greenland or Canadian Inuit Dog
- Icelandic Sheepdog
- Norwegian Puffin Dog
- Nordic Spitz
- Norwegian Buhund
- Corded Poodle

- Spinone Italiano
- Wirehaired Pointing Griffon
- Slovensky Pointer
- Picardy Shepherd
- Bergamasco
- Anatolian Shepherd
- Australian Kelpie
- Kyi Leo
- Shiloh Shepherd

CHAPTER 5

• •

OUTFITTING YOUR MUTT

You've found the perfect dog or puppy! But what are you going do when you bring him home? Where will he sleep? What will he eat? What toys will he play with? Along with your dog comes—dog supplies. And it's best to be prepared before you bring Rover home.

In 2001, pet owners spent $28.5 billion on their pets, and the pet supply industry has grown to meet the increasing demand. With the myriad of toys, leashes, collars and other stuff, you may think buying supplies for your new mutt is a simple enough task. However, many well-meaning dog owners buy the wrong items. For example, there are many unsuitable toys for dogs that are sold in dog supply stores because they have mass appeal for the unaware dog owner.

WHERE TO BUY

The way to avoid the hype and the expense is to buy your mutt's supplies before you bring him home, so that you won't be scrambling to buy things at the last minute. Last-minute purchases usually cost more and offer less quality.

If you have a few weeks to plan, you may be able to save some money by buying your pet equipment from a catalog or an Internet site. Many good mail order pet supply companies provide inexpensive, reliable service—but be wary of the shipping charges! It won't help you much if the dollars you save are eaten up by shipping and handling.

The downside, of course, is if you need the equipment now or within a few days. Some mail order or Internet order companies may ship next day at a higher cost, often canceling the savings. You also cannot examine the product closely to determine if it is really what you want.

WHAT TO BUY

Large pet supply stores sometimes offer discounted items, but you may also find their prices to be higher than you expected. Shop around if you can.

So, what do you really need? Here is a short list of supplies you should buy before your dog comes home.

For Your Home

- A crate; it can be either wire or the plastic airline variety, but be sure it has a good latching system. You will need this crate for housetraining and to keep your mutt in a safe place when you are unable to watch him. The crate should be large enough for your mutt to stand up, turn around and lie down comfortably. Depending on the age of your dog, you may have to buy a smaller one when he is a puppy and a larger one once he reaches his full height.
- Bed or bedding material (to fit in the crate)
- Fencing, and outdoor kennel or some other outdoor containment system
- Enzymatic cleaner for accidents

Your Mutt's Wardrobe

- Flat or buckle collar
- ID tag with your name, address and phone numbers
- Training collar
- Six-foot leather leash

Eating and Drinking

- Food and water bowls
- Premium dog or puppy food
- Training treats and dog biscuits
- Various chew items and toys

Grooming

- Shampoo and conditioner made for dogs
- Slicker brush or soft brush, depending on your dog's coat

- Flea comb
- Comb
- Nail clippers
- Toothbrush and toothpaste made for dogs

BONES, CHEWS AND OTHER EDIBLE ITEMS

Controversy abounds when it comes to what is safe to give your dog. If you believe all the contradictory statements made by pet owners, on the Internet and in books such as this one, you're likely never to give your dog a toy, bone or chew again. The problem is, nothing is 100 percent safe for your dog to chew, and if there were, he probably wouldn't like it anyway.

The other problem is that dogs absolutely need to chew on things, so simply skipping the chew toys is not an option. So what do you do? Use common sense when purchasing items for your mutt, until you learn what his chewing habits are. Look for items that can't be easily torn apart and always supervise your dog while he is chewing on the toy until it is obvious that he can't easily tear it apart and swallow large pieces—which can present a choking or blockage hazard. Safer toys are usually made from hard rubber or flavored nylon, but tough chewers can snap pieces off or wear them down to nubs.

Rawhides tend to be a favorite with many dogs, but if your mutt is an aggressive chewer, you should watch him carefully. Too much swallowed rawhide can cause an intestinal blockage. If you do decide to give your mutt rawhide, choose rawhide made in the United States to avoid the possibility of diseases and poor handling.

What about bones? Most bones are *not* safe. Don't give your mutt poultry, fish, pork, steak or any other sharp bones. These bones can lodge in the throat and present a choking hazard or perforate an intestine. Even larger bones can cause trouble if they splinter.

The "safer" bones are knucklebones and large marrow bones, but there is controversy surrounding their safety. Freezing them tends to make them tougher, but some veterinarians recommend boiling them to eliminate any bacteria. Again, experts dispute the right course of action. If you do give bones to your mutt, only do it while you can watch him. If he chews off a piece or splinters the bone, take it and all the pieces away from him. Some pet suppliers offer prebasted, precooked bones, but again, it's your call about whether these are safer.

OPTIONAL ITEMS (BUT YOU'LL WONDER HOW YOU MANAGED WITHOUT THEM)

The items in the previous section are the basics; these items will make your life easier and in many cases, may be essential for your mutt's comfort. These not-so-necessary items may actually make you wonder how you did without them for so long

- **Sweaters:** Don't laugh! If you have a short-coated dog or one with a single coat that requires clipping, a sweater will help keep him warm during cold winters.
- **Pooper scoopers:** These work better than a shovel to pick up dog poop.
- **Poop bags:** You can use plastic bags to pick up after your mutt on walks, but they can be flimsy and may have holes in them. The pre-made poop bags are self-sealing and very strong.
- **Clippers and grooming shears:** Essential for touch-ups on single-coated breeds, but it is imperative that you learn how to use these properly or you may injure your mutt.
- **Nail grinders:** Some dogs who can't tolerate having their nails clipped will handle electric nail grinders just fine.
- **Grooming table:** This table will save your back by saving you from bending over all the time. Even if you have a large dog, these are great for grooming. Most owners teach their medium to large dogs to jump up on the table on command.
- **Baby gates:** These gates are very handy for cordoning off areas that are off limits to your dog.
- **Exercise pens or ex-pens:** Dog owners use these pens to confine their dog while they can't watch them. They're portable, so you can bring them with you. Be sure the pen is tall enough so your mutt can't jump or climb out.
- **Blow dryer for dogs:** Once you wash your mutt, drying him so he doesn't get cold is important. Hair dryers made for humans are too hot for a dog's sensitive skin and may burn him.
- **Toys:** Your mutt will consider these vital. Get plenty of toys to keep boredom chewing in check.

- **Retractable leash:** Most owners of small and medium dogs swear by these leashes for walking. Only use them with a well-behaved dog.

- **Litter box and doggie litter:** If you live in an apartment in the city, you may choose to litter train your small to medium dog.

DOG FOOD DOS AND DON'TS

What dog food is best for your mutt? Are all dog foods the same? Should you buy your dog food at Chez Snob Pet Boutique or will supermarket dog food do? What about the food your veterinarian carries? Your neighbor feeds her dogs an all-natural diet of sea kelp, raw meat and granola and tells you that your mutt will die of cancer by three years old if you don't feed that diet. Is she right?

With all the confusing information out there, you may be longing for the days when you simply opened up a bag of food and poured. Well, you still can, but you must do it sensibly. Your puppy or adult dog still needs good nutrition, regardless of breed. Always feed a premium dog food.

But aren't all dog foods the same? Not exactly. Premium dog food has better ingredients and less bulk or non-nutritive ingredients. This means more nutrition in your dog and less waste you have to scoop up. So although a premium food may cost more, you can feed less to your dog and he'll still get the same nutrition.

Choose a dog food in which the first ingredient is a meat source, such as poultry, chicken, pork, meat, meat or poultry by-products or a meat meal (such as chicken meal). Always pick a food that meets or exceeds AAFCO's guidelines. (These foods have a statement on their label that says this.) AAFCO is the Association of Animal Feed Control Officials, who have established minimum requirements for dog and puppy foods. If the pet food does not meet AAFCO guidelines, it can't be labeled as complete and balanced.

Also choose a food that's right for your dog's life stage. In other words, puppies really do need puppy food. Their nutritional needs are different from adult dogs, and puppy food has what they need.

The next step is to find a food that's easily available. You don't want to search all over town for your mutt's food because you ran out on a Sunday night, when your local pet boutique is closed.

Finally, and most important to your mutt, find a food that your dog likes. All the nutrition in the world is useless if your dog won't eat it. (More on nutrition in Chapter 15.)

What about your neighbor's homemade diet? Forget the fad diets. Many fad diets for dogs—mostly, the mix-your-own kind—are dangerously imbalanced. While many dogs look like they may be doing well on them, there can be insidious problems going on beneath that apparently healthy coat. Diet formulation should be left to veterinary nutritionists. But if you're convinced you should formulate your dog's food, consider talking with a veterinary nutritionist who can analyze the diet for deficiencies.

• •

CHAPTER 6

BRINGING YOUR MUTT HOME

Now that you have your mutt properly outfitted, it's time to bring her home. Or is it? Have you dog-proofed your home? Have you chosen a veterinarian yet? Do you know what to do the first few days with your new friend?

The transition can be a positive or a negative experience, depending on how well you've prepared. Learn how to puppy-proof your house and what to do when you get your dog home, and you'll all have much better memories of those first few days.

PUPPY-PROOFING 101

Puppies are destructive little critters. Like with children, it's the very nature of those sweet, oh-so-adorable puppies to explore. Unfortunately, puppies use their mouths to explore, picking up everything. And of course, anything that is picked up gets chewed and swallowed. Consequently, if you have a cluttered home or lots of knickknacks, you're going to have to do some cleaning and rearranging.

Begin by taking a look around your home at a puppy's or dog's eye level. Get on your hands and knees and look for anything that might be tempting. Things with strings or tassels, glittery knickknacks and objects your dog can easily reach are all prime targets. Electrical and curtain cords are also very enticing—and dangerous. Hide them or put them out of reach of inquisitive mouths.

Even if you adopt an adult dog, you don't know your dog's habits. Many dogs are turned in to animal shelters and rescue groups because of behavior problems. Those problems include destructive chewing. For whatever reason, the owners couldn't be bothered retraining their dog.

Decide now where you're going to allow your dog and what areas are off limits. If your mutt is allowed everywhere, be sure you've dog-proofed all areas of your home. Some owners like to start with a few rooms and gradually allow the dog in other rooms in the house. It gives them time to see what the dog will actually get into before allowing her into other rooms in the house.

Inside Your Home

When you look at your home, spend extra time in areas that may present the most hazards, such as the kitchen and bathroom. Anything that has items that can be pulled to the floor and chewed may be a danger. Here is a partial list of items to look for:

- Alcohol: very poisonous to dogs
- Bathroom cleaners, shower cleaners
- Candles
- Children's toys, especially those with small pieces that can be chewed off or swallowed
- Chocolate: extremely toxic to dogs; baking chocolate and dark chocolate are more poisonous than milk chocolate
- Dental floss: can become lodged in the throat or intestines
- Electrical cords
- Garbage pails
- Glass knickknacks
- Houseplants
- Knives
- Medications, including ibuprofen, acetaminophen and aspirin
- Vitamins
- Onions: can cause anemia
- Pennies: can cause "penny poisoning" due to the zinc content
- Pens, paper and other small items that may be chewed or swallowed
- Plates and glasses: can be knocked over
- Scented soaps, potpourri, scented plug-ins and air fresheners
- Sewing needles, craft kits
- Shampoo, conditioner, mouthwash
- Socks: can be chewed or swallowed whole and cause an obstruction

- Other clothing items
- Suntan lotion
- Toothpaste: very toxic to dogs

Your Garage

The garage is full of toxic chemicals such as antifreeze and pesticides, and may have dangerous items such as tools and nails. The garage should be off limits to your dog. But just in case she gets into it, you should keep these items out of reach:

- Antifreeze, windshield washer fluid and other car fluids
- Batteries
- Lawn and garden chemicals
- Mouse and rat poisons; these poisons are also dangerous if your dog eats a mouse or rat that has eaten the poison
- Nails, screws and other hardware that can be ingested
- Paint and paint remover
- Saws and other hand tools that may be sharp

Your Backyard

The backyard can be a source of danger for dogs. Both what you plant and the weeds that grow in the yard can be poisonous. You should also periodically check your backyard for possible hazards and loose areas in your fencing. Other hazards include:

- High decks: dog can jump from them and be injured
- Lawn and garden chemicals: can be absorbed through paw pads or licked off fur
- Mushrooms and fungi: many are toxic or even deadly
- Sharp edging: can cut paws
- Stones: many dogs love to eat small rocks and gravel that can lodge in the intestines
- Swimming pools
- Toxic plants: these are too numerous to list, but include evergreen plants such as holly and pods from the black locust tree; contact your local poison control center or state agricultural office for a list of poisonous plants in your area.

FIRST STOP: VETERINARIAN

Before you bring your mutt home, make an appointment to take her to the veterinarian on the way. This ensures that your dog or puppy is healthy before you bring her home. Some shelters require that you have your puppy checked by a veterinarian within a week after you adopt your dog.

But how do you find the right veterinarian? If you adopt from a shelter, some offer coupons for a free or low-cost checkup that many local veterinarians will accept. You can get a list of veterinarians in your area from the shelter. One of them might even be a favorite of your dog-owning friends. Most dog owners will recommend a local veterinarian they like.

Other resources for finding a vet can include dog trainers or groomers. You can also look in the Yellow Pages in the phone book, contact your state's veterinary association, or contact the American Veterinary Medical Association (AVMA) of the American Animal Hospital Association (AAHA) for a list of veterinarians near you (you'll find contact information for these groups in Appendix A).

Call the veterinarians you are considering. Many clinics offer additional services such as grooming and boarding for their clients. This may be important to you if you have a dog who requires intensive grooming or if you need to board your dog at any time. The following questions will help you decide which veterinarians might be right for you.

- What hours is the clinic open?
- How many veterinarians are in the practice?
- Does the clinic handle emergencies or is there an after-hours number where you can reach the veterinarian or an on-call veterinarian?
- Does the clinic offer boarding?
- Do the veterinarians make house calls?
- Is there a groomer available?
- Do the veterinarians have their own lab equipment or do they need to send out for tests?
- Are the veterinarians specialists? What are they specialists in?
- Is this a clinic or hospital?
- Do the veterinarians offer a multi-pet discount on certain services?

Once you narrow the list, ask to visit the veterinary clinic. Don't drop by unannounced—some days are busier than others. When you visit, look around. Is the staff pleasant and friendly? Is the clinic clean and orderly? Does everything smell okay? If there has been an emergency or if this is a particularly busy day, the clinic might be a little messy, but the overall appearance should leave a good impression.

BRINGING YOUR DOG HOME

Choose a day to bring your dog home when you have time to spend with her, so you can really help her feel wanted and make the adjustment to her new surroundings. Often, this means taking vacation days or time off. If you can't take off time, at least wait until a Friday afternoon to bring her home, so you have the weekend with her.

The worst possible time to bring a dog home is around the holidays. Many shelters will recommend that even if you have picked out a dog, you wait until after the holidays to bring her home—when the guests are gone, there's less trouble to get into and you have time to spend with a dog or puppy.

To bring your dog home, you'll need to have her crate ready in your car. Many dogs become carsick, fearful or worse when riding in the car—a crate keeps your mutt safe and secure in one place while you can focus on driving home. Even if you bring a second person along with you, you should still transport the dog in the crate. Don't trust your passenger to hold your mutt—dogs and puppies can squirm out of people's arms at the most inopportune moments.

Once you get home, put a leash on your mutt and have her walk around outside until she relieves herself. She may be too excited to urinate or defecate at first, so be patient. Let her sniff around and allow her to explore the new area. Once some of the excitement has worn off, she'll have to relieve herself.

You may think that having all your friends and relatives show up for a giant puppy party might be a good idea. It's not. Your canine companion will need some quiet time to adjust to her new surroundings, and too many people will be overwhelming. She'll be overwhelmed as it is with a new owner and a new home—give her time to adjust.

Nor is this the time to introduce your new dog to the rest of your pets (if you have any). Keep your other dogs crated and the cats in another room while your mutt becomes accustomed to you and her new surroundings. When you introduce your new dog to the rest of the pets, it's better to introduce dogs on neutral ground. More on this in the next section.

INTRODUCING THE OTHER FAMILY PETS

Hopefully, you already know whether or not your new dog is good with other dogs or cats. If you've obtained an adult mutt from a shelter, they may have been able to give you some background about the dog you've adopted. If your dog is a puppy, it is crucial for her to be introduced correctly to other dogs and pets.

Other Dogs

If you have another dog, the other dog may look on your mutt as an interloper. Your other dog may behave in unexpected ways, including snarling and biting. Never bring a new dog home and leave her alone with your current dog. You may have a serious dogfight.

Introduce your new mutt and your current dog on leash in a neutral place (not your home or yard), preferably in a park. Have a family member hold the leash of your current dog as you approach with your

*Choosing another dog about the same size and the
opposite sex may cut down on aggression.*

new mutt. Watch for signs of aggression: walking stiff-legged, hackles (the hair on the back of the neck and shoulders) raised, hard stares, lifting or curling the lip, growling or snarling. A little posturing is okay, but correct either dog for aggression.

Be very careful not to hold the leash tightly the first time you introduce the two dogs. You will telegraph your nervous feelings to your dogs and they will pick up on it and become nervous as well.

If you have adopted an adult dog, she may or may not be dog aggressive. At least try to choose a dog of a similar size and the opposite sex, and in any case, never leave the two dogs unsupervised until you are certain that they have become good friends. A much larger dog will outmatch the smaller one if a dog fight ensues.

If your mutt is much larger or smaller than your current dog, you should keep the two dogs separated while alone. Some dogs, breeds and breed mixes are naturally inclined toward aggression and fighting. That tendency will always be there, regardless of training or correction. Don't leave your dogs unsupervised. Either dog may be severely injured or killed.

Introducing the Cat

Some dogs do great with cats; others think cats are dinner. It depends on the individual dog. Dogs with some sighthound or Northern breed in them may have an especially strong prey drive and may want to chase your cat. If your dog is an adult, you should already know whether or not she is good with cats and other pets.

Sometimes dogs and cats get along with very little fuss. This is Zoe and Franklin.

If your mutt is a puppy, you may be able to introduce the family cat to her. Once the cat has swatted them on the nose, many puppies learn to leave the cat alone.

If your mutt is an adult, but is considered good with cats, you can keep your cat in other rooms so your dog can become used to the cat's smell. Once you allow the dog and cat to meet, be certain your cat has a way to get out of the dog's reach in case she gets excited and starts to chase her. Correct your dog for any chasing.

Sometimes teaching your dog to focus on you while the cat is in the room works well. Teach your dog "Watch me!" (see Chapter 11) while the cat is in the room, and give her praise and treats for watching you instead of the cat.

Other Pets

Birds, reptiles, rodents and rabbits should *always* be kept away from your mutt to avoid unfortunate incidents.

HOW TO GET A GOOD NIGHT'S SLEEP

A new dog or puppy will most likely whimper or cry the first few nights. After three nights of no sleep, you may be questioning why you ever fell in love with that oh-so-adorable puppy who is screaming at the top of her lungs even now.

Your mutt should sleep in your bedroom, in a crate, next to your bed. Not in the basement. Not in the kitchen. Not in the empty bedroom. *Your* bedroom. Your mutt needs to feel secure and to bond with you. Even though you may be asleep, your presence will be comforting to your new dog. It's practical too—if your dog has to go out, she can tell you and you can let her out or, if she is just fussing, you can lean over and tap the crate and tell her "No!"

If your mutt is a puppy who has recently left her mother, she may be lonely for her mother and siblings. You can get a hot water bottle, fill it with warm water and wrap it in a towel so your puppy can lie against it. Experts claim that the ticking of an old-fashioned alarm clock imitates the heartbeat of her mom and siblings, but whether this works or not is an individual thing. (Turn off the clock's alarm or you're both in for a rude wake-up!)

The most sensible way to ensure a puppy or dog sleeps through the night is to give her a long walk or exercise her before going to bed. A tired dog is a sleepy dog and one who is less likely to whine during the night. Be certain she relieves herself before putting her in her crate at night.

CHAPTER 7

CRATES AND HOUSETRAINING

People will put up with a lot from their pets. I've seen people have dogs who aren't the slightest bit trained—who have never learned sit, lie down or even how to walk nicely on a leash. But no one puts up with a dog who isn't housetrained.

Housetraining—or housebreaking, as it's commonly called—is vital for any pet. Think about it: How pleasant is it to live in a house that a dog considers to be his toilet? Not very! Even if you fail to train your mutt in anything else, you must teach him to go outside or in a litter box.

How do you do this? You need a crate.

CRATES

A vital tool in housebreaking is the crate. Some people consider this a euphemistic term for "cage," but your dog doesn't see it like that. Most dogs have a natural denning instinct that makes them feel secure while they're confined. If you've ever watched a dog who's afraid of thunderstorms, the first thing you'll see him do is crawl under something—a bed, coffee table, a chair. (I've had three 100-pound dogs cower together under my computer desk during some really bad electrical storms!) In the wild, foxes, coyotes and wolves all seek shelter underground during a storm. While your domesticated dog doesn't have a den in your backyard (or maybe yours does, in which case, check out Chapter 13), you can provide him the same security blanket by giving him the next best thing—a crate.

Most dogs think of their crates as their beds. I've seen my dogs in their crates napping or awaiting me to close the crate when it's their bedtime. However, a few dogs positively despise crates—no doubt due to incorrect use or never having a safe, secure place. In this case, you may have to opt for an ex-pen (an exercise pen, available at pet supply stores) or confine the dog to a small area. Don't give up easily on crates, though. You will have a much harder time training your dog to accept a crate than you will housetraining him without a crate.

Crates come in two styles: wire and plastic travel. (There's a third type that's made of PVC tubes and cloth mesh, but you should avoid those since they're only for dogs who are crate-trained and are intended for obedience and agility shows.)

The wire type looks more like a cage, but allows air to circulate more freely. The plastic travel style is usually the type of crate allowed on airlines (useful if you're planning on traveling with your mutt). Both have their advantages and disadvantages. Whichever you decide on, choose a sturdy crate with a secure latch. Some escape artists have chewed or scratched through crates or reached around to open latches. Choose a crate that is large enough for your dog to stand up, turn around and lie down in.

You will have his crate in your bedroom, but you may want to move it to an area such as your den or living room when you're home but you need to crate your dog. When should you crate a dog? Any time you can't watch him—at least until he's trustworthy enough to be loose in the house. For this reason, having more than one crate—one in the bedroom and one in the kitchen, for example—might be a good idea.

Crate Training 101

So how do you get started crate training? Ideally, you should start by putting your dog in for the smallest amount of time (such as five minutes) and work your way up. Unfortunately, life isn't ideal, is it? What usually happens is that you have to go to work or school, or leave the house, or—heaven forbid!—get some sleep. You slip the puppy in the crate and he cries, annoying your neighbors or keeping you up all night.

That doesn't work either, does it? You need to teach your dog that going into the crate and staying there is a good thing. Don't force your dog to go into the crate. Instead, toss treats into the crate to get him to enter. (If it isn't a good enough treat to lure him in the crate, use something really tempting—a piece of hot dog or cold cuts.) After he's in the crate, give him a toy or a favorite chew. If the chew isn't interesting enough, find one that is. Give him treats for going in the crate. Feed him meals in the crate. Soon, he'll be associating good things with that crate.

Before you put your mutt in the crate for longer periods (bedtime, leaving for work or school, and so on), exercise your dog. Take him for a long walk, play ball with him or horse around in the backyard. Also, make sure he eliminates before you put him in the crate. The idea is to tire out your mutt so all he wants to do is sleep. A sleepy puppy is a happy puppy and one who is not likely to fuss.

If you are leaving for a few hours, turn on a classical music or light jazz station on the radio. Dogs are great at associations, and you'll be teaching yours that classical music means naptime. A favorite trick of mine is to turn the television to the Weather Channel. The format is repetitious and they play light classical or jazz music. My dogs have their own favorite weather forecasters. Avoid television or radio stations with news or talk shows—many have arguments and their voices are stressed or angry. You want a calm puppy, not one who is unhappy and educated in partisan politics!

There are CDs and tapes for latchkey pups, but I've never tried them. One veterinarian I know recommends that her clients read a boring book into a tape recorder and then play it back while they're gone. Your voice will be soothing and will help calm your pup. (This would probably work just as well with an interesting book.)

Use the same command every time to tell your dog to go into the crate. I use the word "bed" or "go to your bed," but I've heard people use "crate" or "place." It doesn't really matter, as long as you use the same word every time; "bed" just sounds nicer.

Crate Training for Older Dogs

Crate training an older dog is much like crate training a puppy. Some older dogs are already crate trained, and if they are, that's great! However, some older dogs are more resistant to crate training because they've never been introduced to crates before. Patience is key here, as are treats and praise. If—for any reason—you can't keep your dog from carrying on in the crate, you may have to resort to an ex-pen.

HOUSETRAINING 101

Housetraining, as I've said, is a very important part of your dog's training. If your dog is a puppy, it may take some time to housebreak him. Some puppies catch on fast; others do not. I've heard of some dogs taking as long as a year to completely housetrain. I've had dogs who have taken nearly that long.

Old, outdated training methods usually work poorly, if at all (see Housetraining Don'ts in this chapter) and may result in a neurotic dog

WHAT TO USE TO CLEAN UP ACCIDENTS

Accidents happen. When your mutt relieves himself in the house, you need to remove all traces of the urine smell or he will continue to relieve himself in that same spot. Fancy cleaners for floors and carpets often have ammonia in them—the same ingredient found in urine! Even if the fancy cleaner doesn't have ammonia in it, the cleaner may not remove the urine smell entirely from the carpet. (Remember, your dog can smell things that you can't.)

So, how do you rid the carpet and floor of urine smell? Once you clean up the mess, use a good commercial brand of enzymatic cleaner especially formulated for pet accidents (available at pet supply stores or on the Internet). Or if you're on a budget or can't find enzymatic cleaner, use a mixture of white vinegar and water to neutralize the odor.

who still urinates on the carpet. Instead, the right approach is a schedule. Your puppy needs to be ushered outside when:

- He first wakes up
- After every meal
- After drinking water
- After exercising
- Before being put into a crate for longer than a few minutes
- After he comes out of the crate
- Before bedtime

This sounds like quite a bit of work, but you will have far fewer accidents this way. You should keep an eye on him when he's loose—puppies will often sniff or circle when they're getting ready to eliminate. If you see that behavior, pick up your pup and take him outside.

When you bring your puppy outside, watch him and praise him for eliminating. Some people like to use a command word such as "go potty!" while the dog is urinating or defecating. Then, the dog knows that when he hears "go potty!" it's time to eliminate.

But how does a crate work into all this? You need to keep your puppy in the crate when you can't watch him. Dogs naturally don't want to eliminate in a place they have to lie in, so they will wait until they are out of the crate. This is why it is important to establish a routine, so your pup knows he won't have to hold it for too much longer. You also should never make a puppy younger than six months stay in a crate longer than four hours, except at bedtime.

When you can't watch your puppy, put him in the crate. It only takes a single moment of inattentiveness for him to piddle on the carpet behind your back.

Many trainers believe that you shouldn't correct a dog for having an accident on the carpet, saying the dog will not associate the correction with the evidence. It's been my experience that you can correct a dog for relieving himself inside, but without all the old, revolting techniques (dragging the dog over, sticking his nose in it and so on). If you catch your puppy in the act, you'll probably gasp or exclaim "No! No!" anyway. Whisk him outside and praise him when he finishes outside. Then clean up the mess with either a good enzymatic cleaner or soap followed with white vinegar and water to eliminate the smell.

If you find the evidence after the fact—a puddle or a pile—pick up your puppy or lead him to the pile and show it to him. In a low voice, tell him "No! This is bad!" Don't hit your dog and don't rub his face in it. Don't yell at him. Just show him the evidence and show how displeased you are. Some trainers believe that dogs have poor memories for these things, but I've found quite the contrary. Dogs have exceptional memories for places and things—I've found my own dogs recognize places from over a year ago.

When you show the pile or puddle, your puppy will probably become submissive when he hears your displeased tone. Bring him outside and wait until he urinates or defecates outside. (Sometimes bringing the pile outside will help your puppy understand where you want him to go.) Praise him when he goes outside. Then clean up the accident with an enzymatic cleaner or soap followed by white vinegar and water.

I can't emphasize enough how patient you must be with your puppy. Many mixed breeds are clever and pick housetraining up quickly, but some are more difficult. Your training methods must be consistent, too. Each time your puppy has an accident in your house, you will have to work harder to prevent the next accident.

Eventually, your puppy will learn to ask to go outside. But sometimes you don't pick up his signal and he may be waiting by the door for a long time. One way to avoid this is to teach him to ring a bell to go out (see the box on page 66).

A Cool Trick

If you hang a bell on the doorknob, it's easy to teach your dog to nose the bell to ask to go outside. Hang the bell at nose height. When your dog needs to go out, stand by the door and wait until he physically noses the bell before opening the door. Most dogs will be so excited that they'll hit it pretty quickly. Smart dogs soon make the association, but even the most stubborn ones figure this trick out if you're consistent. I've actually had some dogs learn to nose the bell by watching or even hearing other dogs nose the bell to go out!

Housetraining the older dog is usually easier than housetraining a puppy. Stick with the schedule and crate your dog when you can't watch him. Most adult dogs can hold it for eight hours, but you may wish to work up from four hours at first. A few times teaching him to eliminate outside is usually all that's needed, and the dog is housetrained.

Housetraining Dos
The best way to housetrain is to:

- Crate your dog when you are unable to watch him.
- Make a schedule and stay with it.
- Praise your dog every time he eliminates outside.
- Use vinegar and water or enzymatic cleaner to clean up accidents.
- Bring plastic bags on walks and clean up after your dog.
- Clean up poop in your backyard at least twice a week. You can compost dog feces and use it on non-food plants (flowers, trees, shrubs) or throw it out.

Housetraining Don'ts
Unfortunately, there's a lot of old knowledge out there. Here are some vital don'ts:

- Don't rub your dog's nose in his accidents.
- Don't paper train.
- Don't whack him with a rolled-up newspaper.

- Don't leave your dog for longer than eight hours in a crate; four hours if he is a puppy.
- Don't restrict water, especially in hot weather.
- Don't force your dog to hold it—take him out.
- Don't use household cleaners to clean up accidents.
- Don't leave your dog in a large area alone.

Why Not Paper Training?

People used to paper train as an intermediate step to housetraining. The idea was to teach the puppy to go on the papers when he couldn't hold it for very long, and eventually graduate him to going outside. The problem with paper training is that it teaches a dog that it's okay to use the house as a bathroom. I made that mistake with my first dog, Conan, who thought he was supposed to go inside, not out! It took nearly a year to fully correct the behavior. Don't paper train—it makes housetraining more difficult.

Litter Box Training

If you own a very small mutt and live in an apartment where it's not practical to bring him outside several times each day, you may wish to consider litter box training. There are now dog litter and dog litter boxes available.

Litter box training is very much like housetraining, but with some important exceptions. First, you will have to put the litter box in a place where your dog can get to it and where you are unlikely to move it. Otherwise, you may find puddles beside the closed door or where the litter box used to be. Second, you will need to clean the box frequently so your home won't smell. And finally, instead of taking your dog outside on a schedule, you will bring him to the box and praise him when he eliminates. You may be able to facilitate training by putting his feces in the box and praising him when he goes. Otherwise, use the same training and the same routine to teach him to eliminate in the box as I have described for housetraining.

Does this teach a dog to go indoors? Yes, and if at all possible, you should avoid litter box training. But if you have no choice, it is an option. Do not teach a dog larger than 30 pounds to use a litter box—the amount of waste makes it impractical.

· ·

CHAPTER 8

PROFESSIONAL TRAINING

Some people's dogs . . .

You know what I'm talking about. Their dogs are a pain to meet. They jump up all over you, they pull on the leash, they won't come when their owners call.

Not your dog, you say. You want a dog with good manners. She should walk nicely on a leash and come when you call. She should greet your friends politely and never steal food off the table. You want her to enjoy rides in the car and not behave like someone's spoiled brat in public. You want a dog who is a joy to be around.

But you're not quite sure about this obedience stuff. After all, you don't require perfect sits and downs that would score a High in Trial in formal obedience competition. Certainly, you can pick up a book (like this one) and train your dog to be a good canine citizen.

SHOULD YOU TRAIN YOUR MUTT?

Well, maybe.

Dog training isn't rocket science, but trying to teach you the nuances of dog training in a book is a little like teaching doctors through correspondence courses. I don't think either you or I would find the results entirely acceptable. If you've trained dogs before, you probably have a good idea what I'm talking about when I describe the "heel position," but you've also gone through some trial and error. You've made mistakes with earlier dogs and either you were able to fix them before they became a problem or the dog was smart enough to compensate. Then again, maybe not.

If you have the time and experience to train your own dog and are willing to work through the mistakes novices make, then go for it. But if you're realistic about your time and know that you don't have the

A well-trained dog is a joy to own. This is Pepper Jubilation,
owned by Rhonda and Daniel Metzer.

patience to study and really teach yourself the right techniques, then look for a professional trainer. After all, most people call a plumber when they need to install a sink and most people send their kids to school instead of teaching them at home. So why do people expect to be experts when it comes to dog training?

LOOKING FOR THE RIGHT TRAINER

Different dogs need different training. Some dogs are "easy"—they're quick learners and pick up on things without much effort. Other dogs are stubborn and independent—they know what you want, but they just don't care to do it. Then there are the clueless—you're speaking a whole other language and they can't understand what you want. Then there are the clueless *and* stubborn . . .

You get the idea. A good professional dog trainer will have seen all of these dogs, and more. But how do you find a good professional dog trainer? Anyone can hang a sign up and call themselves a professional dog trainer.

Start by talking to your dog-owning friends, your veterinarian and the shelter or group where you adopted your dog. Some veterinarians and shelters offer dog training classes. Talk to dog owners who compete in conformation, obedience and agility. These people will know who is a good trainer.

Some community colleges and pet supply stores offer pet training classes, but be careful! Bargain trainers are often no bargain, and not everyone can train certain dogs. If you need a quick puppy socialization class or basic obedience, they'll probably be just fine. But if you have real issues with your pet, such as aggression, you should look for a trainer who is skilled in all types of training.

When you're looking for a professional trainer, look for someone who uses primarily positive reinforcement training techniques. This means the trainer uses food and other motivational items to teach the dog, rather than using harsh corrections or punishments. Most trainers use a combination of positive and negative techniques— dogs really do need to be told when they're doing something wrong—with an emphasis on the positive. However, there are still some trainers who use harsh, coercive techniques in all their training. You should avoid these trainers.

Trainers should be happy to give you a tour of their facility. Ask them what titles they have earned with their dogs in what canine sports, and what types of training they're proficient in. They should be able to show you ribbons and photos from dogs in conformation, obedience, agility or other sports.

When you find a trainer you think you might like, ask if you can watch a class. Most trainers will be happy to have you observe their training. If they don't want you to watch because you might "steal their secrets," look elsewhere. There are no secrets in dog training.

Find a trainer who teaches *you* how to train your dog. It does no good to have a dog who obeys the trainer perfectly but will not respect and obey you.

TYPES OF TRAINING CLASSES

Most trainers offer a variety of classes, including puppy kindergarten, basic obedience, novice training and other classes.

Puppy Kindergarten

Puppy kindergarten is a basic socialization and training course for puppies younger than six months old. Usually it helps teach puppies manners around other dogs and people, and desensitizes them to everyday things such as umbrellas and loud noises. These classes typically teach some basic obedience, such as sit and lie down. Each class is usually an hour long and the course runs six to eight weeks.

Basic Obedience

Basic obedience picks up where puppy kindergarten left off. It focuses on the most common commands that every dog should know: sit, lie down, stay, come, stand still and heel. Occasionally, basic obedience addresses behavioral issues such as destructive chewing, digging and not coming when called. Sometimes these classes are preparation for more advanced classes, such as novice obedience.

Novice Obedience

Novice obedience is intended to prepare dogs for novice level competition in the obedience ring. To obtain a Companion Dog (UCD) title in obedience, dogs must have qualifying scores in three separate obedience trials. In each trial, the dog must complete the following exercises: heeling on leash, figure-eights, sit, lie down, stand-stay, down-stay, sit-stay, sit in front, and finish (a fancy end to the come command). While the American Kennel Club does not allow mutts in obedience competition, the United Kennel Club does.

Other Classes

There are more advanced classes your mutt can take. These include:

- **Agility:** Your dog will learn how to negotiate obstacles for agility competition training.
- **Attention:** Your dog will learn to focus on you instead of other distractions; this helps with training.
- **Canine Good Citizen:** Your dog will learn the 10 basic obedience skills required to pass the AKC's Canine Good Citizen test.
- **Open and Utility:** Your dog will learn more advanced obedience exercises required to earn Companion Dog Excellent and Utility Dog titles.
- **Tracking:** Your dog will learn how to follow a scent and track competitively for tracking titles.

SPECIAL CONSIDERATIONS FOR MIXED BREEDS

Unfortunately, many training classes are geared toward purebreds and purebred dog owners, because the AKC does not allow mixed breeds in competition. However, the UKC and other organizations do (see page 207), and any good trainer will work with a mixed breed as well as a purebred.

If you're planning on doing more than just having a great pet, be certain that the trainer is familiar with UKC, AMBOR and other organizations. In agility, for example, USDAA, NADAC and UKC all allow mixed breeds to compete. You'll find a long list of canine sports and the organizations that allow mixed breeds to compete in Appendix A.

• •

CHAPTER 9

DOG BEHAVIOR 101

WOLVES AND DOGS

Wolves and dogs aren't that different when it comes to behavior. From the most ordinary mutt to the most expensive purebred, dogs are hard-wired for certain behaviors that have been handed down from their wolf ancestry. Even biologists recognize the similarities, and have classi-fied dogs as *Canis lupus familiaris* — which literally means *familiar wolf.*

Consider the wolf. Wolves live in social groups called packs. Individuals within a pack will vary, but every pack has a social hierar-chy. There is a number one male and a number one female in the pack that biologists and behaviorists call an *alpha.* These alphas give the pack their order and are in charge of the pack. These alpha wolves are usually (but not always) the only wolves who reproduce within the pack. The other wolves work toward ensuring the survival of the alpha pair and their offspring.

The other wolves are also ranked within the pack—according to age, sex, strength and health. There will be beta wolves, who are ranked right below the alphas, and other wolves ranked below the beta wolves, clear down to the lowly omega wolf. The alphas get first dibs on the food; the omega wolf gets the scraps.

The pack structure and the alpha pair are a survival strategy for wolves, ensuring that the strongest wolves procreate and survive. It may seem unfair to us, but this strategy has enabled the wolf to survive for thousands of years.

How does this work for the dog? Dogs have this same hierarchy hardwired in their brains. Some dogs are naturally born with alpha ten-dencies. Others are more easygoing and are willing to be beta or below.

Still others, like the omega wolves, have no self-esteem. Most dogs are naturally somewhere between alpha and omega in personality.

However, dogs are very different than wolves in one important personality aspect: Because of domestication, they've become the Peter Pans of wolves. Their personalities are like those of juvenile wolves. This trait, called *neoteny,* enables dogs to bond with people more easily and to accept humans as alpha.

A dog naturally looks at you as part of his pack. Because of his juvenile personality, he expects you to become his alpha. If you do not, he must be alpha. That puts him in a precarious position—one he really doesn't want to be in. It doesn't make him feel secure when he's in charge and, like a dictator with too much power, he tries to control everything and becomes neurotic.

I'm sure you've seen the spoiled dogs I'm talking about. They clearly rule the roost but are nervous, hyper and yappy about everything. These dogs aren't happy, because their owners have failed to provide the security of knowing that the people are in charge.

HOW TO SPEAK GOOD DOG

So, becoming alpha is not so great for your dog, but is a good thing for you. But how do you go about it? First you must learn to speak good dog. Most of us aren't bilingual when it comes to our dogs—we don't know what they're saying. We constantly mistake being aggressive for being happy because we see a tail wag, or we think our dogs are feeling guilty when they're really acting submissive.

Dogs speak using their bodies, eyes, scents and vocalizations. Because they have no verbal or written language, they also do a lot of observing. They've already figured out when *we're* happy, sad, angry or frightened. They also have ways to tell us when they feel that way—if only we understood.

While many clever dogs can figure out how to communicate what they want to humans—and if you think about it, those dogs who learned how must be canine Einsteins!—most dogs are locked into their canine way of communicating. But it's not that hard to speak dog.

Watch your dog as he reacts to you, other people and other dogs. Is he stiff-legged with a tail straight up? He's being aggressive. Is he wiggly and low, ears back, wagging his tail? He's being submissive. Is he relaxed and bowing, with his tail wagging furiously and a big smile on his face? He's happy and playful. Sometimes the cues can be subtle, such as in aggression, where all you might see is a slight raising of the hackles or a quick snarl. But if you look and understand, you'll see them.

When trying to determine what a dog is feeling, look at the entire dog, not just parts of him. People often think dogs only use their tails to express emotions. While they *do* use their tails, what they are *saying* with their tails depends on the rest of the dog.

So, what is a dog saying? Let's consider different scenarios. You're walking your dog on a leash. Suddenly, another dog comes bounding toward him and stops. That dog is:

- Barking loudly
- Stiff-legged
- Making eye contact with your dog
- Wagging his tail and holding it straight up like a flag
- Perking his ears forward in attention

This is aggressive behavior. You might recognize it as such if the dog is snarling and has his hackles up. But not all dogs do that. The barking could be fear or dominance, but the stiff-legged stance, the eye contact, the forward set to the ears and the tail all say, "Watch out!"

How about a dog who barks and maintains his distance? This is a dog who is exhibiting some guarding behaviors, but is not bold enough to take the challenge head-on. The dog is saying, "Don't make me go over there and beat you up!" but it's mainly a bluff. If you or your dog act fearful or push his comfort zone by challenging this dog, he may become more aggressive.

Let's say you see an unknown dog and, for some reason, you decide to approach him. His body language is:

- Crouched
- Tail tucked between his legs
- Eyes avoiding you
- Teeth clacking
- Ears flattened or drawn back

This dog is clearly submissive! The teeth clacking indicates nervousness and possibly even fear. He may or may not respond to your

ANTHROPOMORPHIZING DOGS

It's natural for us humans to ascribe human emotions to other things. We say the sky looks "angry" when there's a thunderstorm or that the sun is "smiling" on us. We also do this with our dogs. But dogs, by their very nature, have no concept of right and wrong in a moral sense, nor do they feel guilty about a particular action.

A friend demonstrated a graphic example of this. She had her dog sit and praised her. Fair enough. Now my friend pointed to her dog and said, "No, bad dog!"

What do you think happened? The dog, seeing her owner displeased, became submissive, or "looked guilty." But what was she feeling guilty about? Nothing. The dog simply reacted to the angry tone of her owner's voice.

If your dog is used to raiding the table for food, he doesn't feel guilty about doing it. He will become submissive in your presence, knowing that your action will be one of displeasure, but he doesn't feel the slightest bit guilty that he ate the roast. In fact, the roast was quite a reward, and he might cruise the table for dessert later if you're not looking.

kneeling down and talking softly to him. Don't go to him; see if he might come to you. Watch for any aggressive behavior.

Let's look at a happy dog now. Suppose you're playing ball with your dog and he's happily retrieving. You'll see the following:

- Ears are up or flattened, depending on what mood he's in at the moment.
- Body is relaxed.
- Tail is wagging at mid-height.
- Paws may be lifted in an invitation to play.
- Eyes are playful and soft.
- There's a smile on his face.

HOW TO BECOME ALPHA

So, how do you become alpha? Alpha doesn't mean bully your dog or hit or choke him. It doesn't mean rolling him upside down until he urinates submissively and it doesn't mean shaking him by the ruff. What it means is that you must take charge of your dog and establish that you're someone to look up to and respect.

Some trainers don't like the term *alpha* because some people assume it means "be a bully." But being a bully doesn't show your dog that you're someone to respect, it shows your dog that you're someone he should dislike and fear. That's not alpha!

You establish respect by acting like you're in charge. All good things come from you—they don't magically appear in the food bowl or in his crate, you put them there. You set realistic limits and enforce them every time. You're someone your dog looks up to and can feel confident that no matter what the situation, you're in control.

Nowhere is the role of alpha more important than with working dogs. If you're planning on doing any competitive sports or work with your dog—and mutts *do* work—you must establish a partnership between you two. There may be times when your dog must trust you implicitly or else he may get injured (sled dogs, search and rescue dogs, and herding dogs fall into this category). If the dog accepts that you're alpha, he will often defer to your judgment even in a dangerous or scary situation.

ENFORCE YOUR ALPHA ROLE

There are many things you can do to say to your dog, "I'm alpha." One thing is to enforce all rules, no matter how hard your dog tries to get away with something. For example, if you don't want your dog sleeping on the couch, you must stop him from getting up on the couch every single time. You can't let him snuggle with you on the couch one night while you two watch old movies together, just because you feel like it. Either he's allowed on the couch or he's not.

One big mistake I see all the time are owners who call their off-leash dog to come before the dog has been properly trained. The dog doesn't respect his owner, or sees something more interesting, and ignores the command—or worse yet, plays a quick game of "catch me if you can." Not only is this embarrassing, but it can be dangerous. The dog could run across the street and be hit by a car or run away and become lost. Even the cleverest and most well-trained dogs can lose their common sense in the exciting freedom of being unrestricted. And the dog has now learned that he can ignore his owner's commands with no consequences.

Who's in charge of this situation? The hapless owner or their dog? Who looks like alpha now? The owner could have prevented this entire situation by having their dog on a leash until the dog was trustworthy off leash. Even then, many dog owners with well-trained dogs will not risk taking their dogs off leash except under very controlled circumstances.

To Free-Feed or Not to Free-Feed

You need to let your dog know where his treats and food are coming from. That means no free-feeding—dumping his kibble in a big bowl and letting him eat whenever he wants.

If you currently free-feed, you may be thinking you don't have time to fix your dog two or three meals a day, every day. Really? How long does it take to measure out a few cups of kibble in a bowl and set it down? Not even five minutes. Certainly, you can take five minutes out of your busy day to do this.

When you start feeding your dog regular, measured meals, you'll want to have him sit nicely while you fix his food. Once you put his food down, you can release him. The idea here is to make him work for his meal (hold a sit-stay) until you release him (say "okay"). He's focused on you now as the food *provider*—not just focused on the food bowl.

There are other good reasons for not free-feeding, including helping your dog maintain his proper weight. But there's an even more important reason for feeding your dog on a schedule: If he decides to skip a meal, it will alert you that he may not be feeling well. Most dogs, if they're not picky eaters, won't turn away from their meal unless they're feeling sick. If you free-feed your dog, you might not realize he's sick until he's much worse.

When you give your dog treats, you should also make him earn them. Have him sit, dance, yodel—whatever—for his treat. I insist that my dogs at least sit nicely for a treat and take the treat *gently* out of my hand.

Strictly Off Limits

Make your bed off limits to your dog. He needs to sleep in his own bed—preferably in a crate next to your bed. You don't sleep in his bed, do you? Sleeping in your bed together makes you equals.

It's also not a good idea to allow a dominant dog to lie on the other furniture, even if you don't care about it. Again, it puts you on an equal level with your dog, when you should be ranking above him.

Never allow your dog to loom over you or mount you, and don't roughhouse or play tug-of-war games. Allowing your dog to loom over you or mount you puts you in a submissive position. Roughhousing and playing tug-of-war puts you on his level and if you lose tug-of-war, you've just lost to him—and taught him to use his strength against you. Think about it.

Keep Playing Those Mind Games

Alpha wolves eat first, lead the pack and never put themselves in compromising positions with other pack members. How does this translate into what you should be doing?

If your mealtimes coincide, eat your dinner before feeding your dog, like the alpha you are. When you both leave a room, you leave first, followed by your dog. *You* are leading, not him.

Spend five minutes a day training your dog. Just five minutes, no more. It will help tune up his commands and remind him that you're the one-who-must-be-obeyed. Likewise, practice long sit-stays and long down-stays. (You can do this while you're watching television or reading a book.)

Being alpha means being in control. Never give a command you aren't willing—*or able*—to enforce. Otherwise, your dog has just figured out a way to make you less than alpha.

A QUICK ALPHA LIST

- No free-feeding.
- Enter and exit all rooms before your dog.
- Eat your dinner first, before feeding your dog.
- Never give a command you aren't willing or able to enforce.
- Practice commands five minutes a day, every day.
- Practice sit-stays and down-stays.
- No tug-of-war or roughhousing games.
- Never allow a dog to mount you or loom over you.
- Never allow your dog to sleep on your bed.
- Make your dog earn his treats.

RECOGNIZING DOMINANCE AGGRESSION

Aggression has many forms: prey, fear, guarding, competition, frustration and a host of others. Aggression can be caused by a variety of things, including pain, fear, competition and dominance. Dominance aggression seems to give people the most trouble.

It starts with minor infractions. Your dog grumbles when you tell him to get off the bed. He growls when you come close to his food. He ignores a command he knows well, or suddenly starts lifting his leg inside the house. At first, they may seem like little things. But little things quickly become big things if they're not corrected now.

If your dog is snappy when you touch him or if he's lifting his leg in the house, your first action is to bring your dog to the veterinarian for a checkup. Pain makes dogs grumpy, and urinary tract infections can cause your dog to forget his housetraining. Tell your vet what you're seeing and have him thoroughly examine your dog. If your veterinarian doesn't find a biological cause, start implementing the alpha list (see the box on page 79).

If your dog isn't spayed or neutered, do it now. There is no reason you should have an intact mutt! Not only will you help prevent unwanted litters, but you will also help curb hormonal causes of aggression in both males and females.

Dominance behavior comes partly from excessive energy. Exercising your dog daily will help release some of that pent-up frustration. Find a sport you both enjoy, such as agility, flyball, flying disc or freestyle. Not only will you both have fun, but you'll be building the bond between you.

EXERCISE AND ACTIVITIES

Most canine behavioral problems stem from boredom. If your dog has nothing to do, he'll think up something to fill those idle hours. Unfortunately, it may not be what you want him to do.

Dogs are happiest when they have a job to perform. Most dogs love something that keeps them busy: backpacking, agility, tracking or flyball are good examples. A tired dog is a happy dog, and one who is less likely to get into mischief.

Work on basic obedience commands every day, and work on the "watch me!" command (see Chapter 11). If your dog isn't focusing on you but on destructive behavior (chewing, thieving and so on), try tethering your dog to you (see Chapter 13). Finally, work on maintaining your alpha position.

If, at any time, you become fearful or afraid of your dog, contact a professional dog trainer or behaviorist for advice. Most can help you identify what you're doing to encourage your dog's behaviors and what to do to stop them.

CHAPTER 10

DOG TRAINING 101

Training your mutt will make her a more pleasant companion, both at home and in public. A well-behaved dog is more welcome than one who is out of control. Well-behaved dogs are more likely to be invited back. They are canine ambassadors.

Your dog doesn't have to have obedience-title responses to commands to be well-behaved. She doesn't need to know how to fetch or catch a ball in midair (but you can teach her that, if you want). She doesn't need to be perfect—just good enough. Many owners find that knowing how to walk nicely on leash, come when called, sit and lie down on command, and stay is all a house pet needs.

But, as you can guess, different mixed breeds have different issues concerning training. Whether your mutt is a puppy or an adult, and what breeds your dog has in her, will influence what kind of training will work and what kind will not. You'll need to take into account your mutt's own personal style.

TRAINING AN ADULT DOG AND TRAINING A PUPPY

There are pluses and minuses to training puppies and adults. Most puppies have little "baggage"—they haven't been taught something incorrectly and you don't have to fix a problem. However, puppies may take longer to become more proficient at a command, because, well, puppies are puppies. We don't expect children to learn everything all at once, nor do we expect them to learn as quickly and in the same way as adults do. A puppy will need more repetition before she can have the same proficiency as an adult.

When training an adult dog with an unknown history, be aware that the dog may have excess baggage. Maybe she's been trained poorly or maybe she hasn't been trained at all. Maybe her former owners have allowed her to get away with everything. Maybe they've allowed behaviors that you don't approve of. Then again, maybe she had good owners who trained her, but in a way that's different from your style. In most cases, shelter dogs have not been abused, they were just not trained and were allowed to get away with a lot. However, some dogs *have* been abused and some training methods may trigger fearful or aggressive responses.

For example, one dog I found on the street was terrified of having his collar held—not jerked or pulled roughly, simply held. He became even more fearful if you led him around by the collar, regardless of how gently you did it or the fact that the collar was flat and non-slip. This dog probably had some strict training with the collar. Perhaps his previous owner dragged him to whatever he did wrong. I got around his fear by putting him on a short leash and not touching his collar.

When your mutt acts contrary to the way you think she should behave—stop! Especially if she becomes fearful or aggressive. Stop and diffuse the situation. Analyze what you're doing to bring out this unexpected behavior and see if there are alternatives to the method you're using. Try training in a way that is less direct or intimidating. For example, if you're teaching the "down" command and your dog doesn't like having her shoulders touched, try sitting her with her back to a wall and using a treat to lure her to lie down.

TRAINING DIFFERENT KINDS OF MUTTS

What breeds your dog has in her ancestry may also make a difference in how you train her, and how easy it is to get her well trained. How do you know if your dog may be more difficult to train? The only way to know for sure is to work with your dog. If she doesn't get it after several attempts, try another style of training.

Some dogs are motivated by food; some are motivated by toys. If neither of these things inspires your dog to work for you, find something she loves to do and use that as a motivation. For example, I had a dog who was not motivated by praise or food (there are some out there!), but he loved to pull a sled. His motivation was pulling and I used that as an incentive in my training.

No dog is perfect. Your dog may be terrific at sits and downs, but may need work on not pulling on the leash. Some dogs are naturally inclined to pulling hard (Northern breed mixes); others may have trouble sitting for long periods of time (giant breed mixes). Others may be perfectionists (shepherd mixes) who will sit where you want them to and patiently wait for your next command. Each breed is different, and with each breed added to your dog's ancestry, she has a little bit of that character in her. Keep those qualities in mind when you train, but realize that the blend will make your dog's personality unique.

SECRETS OF PROFESSIONAL TRAINERS

- **Never get angry at your dog.** If you feel yourself becoming angry or frustrated with your dog—stop. Take a time out. Stop training. Play with your dog, take a walk or read a book. Don't take your frustration out on your canine partner.

- **Become a person your dog will respect.** Don't yell and scream when she does something wrong. Don't wheedle and cajole her to obey a command. Corrections and praise should be swift, direct and meaningful to the dog.

- **Always reward your dog for coming to you.** Never punish a dog when she runs away and then comes back, or you will be punishing the dog for coming back.

- **Never force a frightened dog to do anything.** You will most likely get bitten.

- **Teach your dog to pay attention to you.** You can do so with food and the "watch me" command.

- **Before you can teach a command, you must first have your dog's attention.** Always precede the command with your dog's name, such as "Shadow, come!" Don't say, "Come, Shadow!" Shadow is likely to have not heard the command before you got her attention.

- **Say the command once. Don't yell.** Shadow is not deaf (if she is, yelling won't help).

- **Don't repeat a command.** You'll be teaching Shadow that she can wait until you say the command several times before she complies. The one exception to this rule is when you are teaching the command the first time.

- **Choose one command and stick with it forever.** Don't say "Shadow, down!" and then "Shadow, lie down!"

- **Choose one-word commands that don't sound like each other.** "Sit down" and "lie down" are perfect examples of commands that will confuse your dog. Use "sit" to mean "sit down" and "down" to mean "lie down."

- **Don't use "down" for "off."** "Down" should mean lie down. "Off" should mean four paws on the ground.

- **Never give a command that you cannot enforce.**

- **Always enforce a command.**

- **Always reward good behavior.**

- **Always set your dog up for success and never allow your dog to make a mistake.** Think through what you are training Shadow to do and what possible responses she can have. Be prepared for all the possibilities.

- **It is easier for a dog to learn good habits than it is to unlearn bad ones.**

- **Always end a training session on a positive note.**

- **Take time to play, especially after a training session.** Shadow needs some playtime with you to release stress and excess energy.

TRAINING EQUIPMENT

You'd never think of going to school without a notebook and a pencil, but people insist on training dogs without the proper equipment. Think of your dog's training collar and the right leash as your dog's way of taking notes—and in a way, they are. These tools are one way you will communicate with your dog.

Training Collars

In addition to your dog's regular flat or buckle collar, you'll need a special training collar. This collar should only be on your dog when you're training her. *Never leave a training collar on your dog while you are not training her, and never use a training collar as a substitute for a flat collar.* Training collars can snag on something and choke your dog, if left on her while she is unsupervised. Never put tags or anything else on a training collar, because these can also snag and cause choking.

There are three standard types of training collars: the slip collar (and limited slip), the snap choke and the prong collar.

Slip Collar

The slip collar—often called a "choke chain"—is a common training collar. "Choke chain" is clearly a misnomer, because no reputable trainer would ever advocate choking your dog! Unfortunately, people have used these training collars incorrectly in the past, giving them a bad reputation.

The slip collar can be made of chain, cord or nylon. It comes in two types: full or limited slip. A full slip collar goes around the dog's neck and tightens as you pull on it. It does not have a stop, so it can continue to tighten.

The limited slip collar tightens to a point, but no further. You see these types of slip collars in showrings, with dogs with delicate necks such as sighthounds, or with sled dogs. This kind of collar provides more control than the conventional flat collar without having the collar tighten too much.

Snap Choke

A snap choke is similar to the slip collar, except that it is made from parachute cord and snaps on a loose ring to provide a tight fit. The snap choke provides positive control, and some trainers use it to handle hard-pulling dogs. Only use a snap choke under the supervision of a professional trainer.

FITTING A TRAINING COLLAR

All training collars should fit close around the neck, preferably high on the neck, just under the jaw. There should be no excess collar dangling—if there is, the collar is too long. Most trainers will help you fit a training collar on your dog.

If you use a slip or limited slip collar, you should make certain it forms a P when you put it on your dog. (If it is a backwards P, it will not release when you snap it, and will continue to tighten, thus choking your dog.)

Prong Collar

The prong collar looks like a medieval torture device. Sometimes called a "pinch" collar, it's made from links of steel that have two prongs per link facing inward. While they look evil, prong collars are actually humane, and they are made so that they can't choke a dog the way a full slip collar can.

Prong collars are used for extremely stubborn and hard-pulling dogs. Unlike with a slip collar, you don't need much strength to use a prong collar effectively. Dogs who pull like a member of the winning Iditarod team get a pinch from their collar every time, and suddenly walk nicely.

But are these collars painful? When the dog pulls against the prong collar, the prongs pull inward. The action doesn't choke, it presses. I've put a prong collar on my arm and snapped it hard. The prongs dug in, but caused me no pain. Even so, only use a prong collar under the supervision of a professional trainer.

Leashes

The very best leash for training is a six-foot leather leash. Don't buy nylon leashes, even though they're cheaper, unless you have a small dog or one who doesn't pull a lot. Nylon can cut your hands and you will have very little control over your dog. Likewise, pass up the chain leashes and other fancy leashes. Get a leather leash—your hands will thank me.

Retractable leashes have grown popular, because they allow a dog to get 10 to 15 feet away and still be on a leash. The problem is that the handles for those leashes don't really give you control, and if the long line tangles around anything, you're in for a mess. If two retractable leashes tangle while your dog is playing with another dog, nothing short of a pocketknife is going to free your two dogs if they get into a fight.

Retractable leashes do have their place. They are excellent tools for teaching "come." Some toy and small dog owners love these leashes, and that's okay because their dogs require little strength to handle.

If you like the idea of a long leash but your dog is likely to pull apart a retractable leash, consider a long line or tracking lead. They're usually made of cotton or nylon and extend 10 to 30 feet. They're often called tracking leads because people who compete in tracking use them to allow their dogs greater maneuverability. Tracking leads are great for teaching "come" and can be a precursor to off-leash work. You can find them on the Internet or at most pet supply stores.

Clicker

Clicker training has become a popular training method in recent years. If you want to try this method of training, you'll need a clicker and a book that explains the method. You can buy both at pet supply stores or directly through clicker guru Karen Pryor's web site at www.karenpryor.com.

Bait Pouch

No, not for fishing! "Bait" is the word dog show people use for treats. These pouches either clip to your belt or have a strap that you clip around your waist. It's a way to protect your pants pockets from smelling like liver or hot dogs.

Treats

Absolutely vital for training—just ask your dog! Choose a variety of treats your dog likes. If it's dog biscuits and commercial treats, fine. But if your dog turns up her nose at those, try tiny bits of cheese, hot dogs, cold cuts and liver. Don't give large pieces of anything. Just a taste will be a good reward. One hot dog should get you through an entire training session or more with a large dog.

BASIC OBEDIENCE COMMANDS

Now that you have your equipment, you're ready to start traning. But how to start? Begin training in short, fun sessions, no more than 15 minutes at a time, and spend some time playing at the end of each session. Pick a command you wish to work on and practice it with your dog. During the next session, review the command your dog has already learned and then teach something new.

Regardless of your progress, keep the training upbeat and positive. If your dog is having trouble learning a command, end on a positive note by having her perform a command she does know, and then stop. Now reward her with a play session!

As your dog becomes more proficient in various commands, try the commands in other places. Have her do the commands both indoors and out, while on leash and while off leash (but within arm's reach). Try her without distractions first and then slowly add distractions. If, at any time, she has problems with a command, go back to a situation where she can succeed. Then build on that success.

Walk Nicely on a Leash

Every dog needs to learn how to walk on a leash without pulling. If your dog has never been on a leash before, put the training collar on her and clip the leash to the training collar. Have a handful of treats in your pocket when you begin walking with her.

At first, she may whirl around you or start pulling. Take a treat out of your pocket and use it to lure her into the proper position, so she isn't pulling on the leash. Praise her and give her the treat when she focuses on you instead of pulling.

Now, walk just a step or two. If she forges ahead or lags behind, a gentle tug on the leash is all it takes to bring her back to where you want her to be. Whenever she walks nicely, tell her, "Good girl!" and give her a treat. As she starts walking nicely, you can slowly reduce the amount of treats and increase the number of steps you take and the verbal praise.

Sit

"Sit" is a useful command when you want your dog to be still. To teach sit, start by holding a treat just above your dog's nose. Bring the treat up and over, behind her head while gently pushing down on her rear end, and give her the command "sit!" When she sits, give her the treat and praise her. Practice this several times and she should sit on command. Vary the reward between treats and praise.

At first, you will be giving the command to sit while you are close to your dog. Once she understands the command, you can clip a leash on her and work at a short distance away from her. With each success, give her praise and treats. If, at any time, she fails to perform a sit correctly, go back to a distance at which she had success and practice there for a while.

Down

Once you teach your dog to sit, you can teach her to lie down. Start by putting your dog into a sit and clip a leash to her collar. Hold a treat in front of her nose, and then lower it to the floor, while gently pulling her collar downward. Give her the command "down!" Give her the treat and praise her each time she succeeds.

Some dogs find this command particularly threatening, because it puts them in a submissive position. If this is the case, try teaching "down" with your dog sitting next to the wall. (Her rear should be touching or almost touching the wall.) Use a treat to lure her down by starting at her nose and bringing the treat down and *toward* her chest. Give her the command "down!" She should have to lie down to get at the treat. Give her the treat and praise her for such a good down!

Stay

The next command your dog should learn is stay. Put her leash on and ask her to sit beside you. Tell her "stay!" and use a flat, open palm in front of her face for emphasis. Take a step or two away and turn to face her. If she tries to move, tell her, "No, stay!" and put her back in position. It usually takes the dog a few times to learn that you want her to stay. Keep her in the stay position for a few seconds, then return to her, release her with "okay," and praise her and give her treats.

Practicing Sit-Stay and Down-Stay

Practice stay in both the sit and down positions. You can slowly lengthen the amount of time or the distance of the stay, but do not add to both at the same time. At the beginning, 20 seconds is a great stay! If she gets up during the stay, decrease the amount of time or distance until she stays reliably. Only increase the distance or time when she is staying reliably.

You don't necessarily need to set aside training time to practice sit-stays and down-stays. Any time is a good time for practicing stays. When you're watching television, reading a book or surfing the Internet are all good times to practice sit-stays and down-stays. Have your dog sit and wait in a stay when you're fixing her food, too.

"Okay," the Release Word

But wait! How does your dog know the sit-stay or a down-stay is done? Most trainers like to use the word "okay" to release a dog from the stay. It's an easy word to remember, and I guarantee your dog will figure this out after only a few times. My dogs look expectantly every time my lips start forming the letter "O."

To release your dog from a stay, say in a happy voice "Shadow, okay!" Then praise a good performance. If your dog still holds the stay, a quick pat will convince her to break it. After a couple of stays, your dog will be waiting for the release word, too.

Come

Come is the most important command you can teach your dog. There may be times when your dog *must* come to you or there will be serious consequences. Suppose your dog accidentally gets out? Will she come to you if you call her? Having a reliable recall may mean the difference between being hit by a car and being safe at home.

Start by clipping a six-foot leash to your dog's collar. Put her in a sit-stay and walk out to the length of the leash. Hold a treat in one hand and call your dog, "Shadow, come!" If she does not come, show her the treat and gently reel her in. When she arrives, give her the treat and praise her. Practice this several times each day.

Once your dog is reliably coming on a short leash, it's time to increase the distance. Now you will need a long line or a retractable leash. Follow the same procedure as you did using the six-foot leash. If your dog doesn't come immediately, reel her in and shorten the distance next time. Always give her a treat regardless of whether you had to reel her in or whether she came without that prompt.

Off-leash recalls can be tricky with some breeds. Practice in a fenced-in area where your dog can't escape. Bring her favorite treat or toy and put her in a sit-stay. Start from six feet away and call your dog, giving her the treat or toy when she comes. If she does not come or dashes away, do not chase her. Either lure her over with treats or walk away. Most dogs will come around to see what you are doing, and then you can catch her. When you do catch her, do not yell or punish her. You should always praise and reward her for coming to you. Then practice recalls on a leash again for another two weeks.

Do not let your dog loose in an open area where she can get away from you until you are certain she will not bolt. Even top trainers don't like to let their dogs loose, because it only takes one time and their dog is gone.

Heeling on a Leash

The correct position for your dog to heel, sit and lie down is beside you, on your left side, facing forward. This is known as the heel position. When you walk your dog, your left hand should loosely hold the leash to control the dog, with any excess leash looped in your right hand. This will give you the maximum control over the dog—even a large or strong one.

To put your dog in the heel position, move your dog to your left side. Use a one-word command such as "place" or "heel" to mean "go to the heel position." When she stands or sits for a few moments in the heel position, give her a treat and praise her. Practice putting your dog in the heel position and reward her when she stands or sits straight in that position. Do not reward sloppily performed commands. Try again and give your dog the treat when she is in the proper position.

Once Shadow knows the heel position, you can teach her to heel. Your dog should be sitting in the heel position with her training collar and leash on. Have a treat in your left hand. Say, "Shadow, heel!" and start walking, left foot forward. If your dog starts to forge ahead or lag behind, get her attention by showing her the dog treat and then lure her into the correct position. When she is in the right position, praise her and give her a treat. If she lags because she is unsure, pat your leg and encourage her to come beside you. Likewise, if she forges ahead, pull her back using the leash or have her focus on the treat and lure her back. Give her the treat when she is in the proper position.

When you stop, have her sit in the heel position and give her a treat. When you start again, always start out on your left foot. Dogs see the left leg movement before the right leg moves, and will take this as their cue to heel.

• •

CHAPTER 11

HOUSE MANNERS

Commands are great, but what about everyday living with a dog? None of the commands you taught your dog in Chapter 10 address things such as table manners or whether it's okay for your dog to lie on the couch. But day-to-day behavior is as important as obedience training. After all, if your dog is raiding your cabinets and destroying your things, whether or not he can sit on command is the least of your worries.

The truth is, preventing bad habits from developing is almost always easier than trying to correct a behavior after it has begun. Before you allow your dog free run of the entire house, start thinking about what should be off limits. Maybe you don't care about the ratty old couch and don't mind if he sleeps on it, but you will feel differently if you buy a new couch. Maybe it's okay if he chews on your son's stinky sweat-shirt and sneakers, but will he know the difference between them and your evening dress and $200 shoes?

Size *does* matter. What is cute or funny from a puppy may annoy or irritate you when the dog becomes an adult. Decide now what is acceptable and what isn't—for the life of the dog. Once you figure out what is acceptable, you can establish some basic house rules.

That said, your dog's behavior is largely up to you and how per-missive you wish to be. Some people like having brats who rule the roost, and think it's cute if their dog growls or chews up their furniture. Others want a nicely behaved dog, but don't mind it if their dog hops on the couch or the bed. Others want a very well behaved dog who stays in certain rooms and doesn't ever climb on the furniture.

While you and I might not think the growling dog is ideal, I'm sure someone out there does, and if that makes this person happy and their dog never bites anyone, I guess it's okay. But most of us fall somewhere between extremely permissive and strict. Just make sure everyone in your family knows the rules, and make sure your dog knows them, too.

LEAD US NOT INTO TEMPTATION

Out of sight, out of mind—that's the dog's philosophy. If he can't see it or get at it, he can't get into trouble with it. I've talked about puppy and dog-proofing in previous chapters, but there are plenty of things your dog can get into without really trying. Kitchen counters, tables and stuff that is just beyond nose reach can easily become *within* nose reach without a lot of effort. Even a slow and docile pup can be motivated to grab a roast off the counter. And once your dog has his reward, he'll remember it. Guaranteed.

So look at what you're doing from a dog's perspective. Is the hot apple pie or Sunday's meat loaf going to tempt him? Do your shoes sit right next to the rawhide chew toy on the floor? What about those chocolate chip cookies? That trash smells interesting since you left the chicken bones from last night's dinner in it. Leaving stuff on the counter or out in the open guarantees a temptation that most dogs can't resist.

Many dog owners have discovered that ovens and microwaves make dog-proof safes for their dinner or food. Cabinets with childproof latches can keep most inquisitive noses out of food areas, and there is always the cupboard, pantry or bathroom for the trash. Or get a trash can with a snap-lock mechanism for the lid.

Ice cream is indeed a dangerous temptation!

If you can't hide the interesting stuff—you have a party at your house, for example, and you have trays of food out— consider putting your pup in his crate until the temptation is gone. It's easy and he won't snatch the deviled eggs—or the angel food cake.

There are static mats and gates available for teaching boundaries. The static mats give an unpleasant sensation just like the static electricity shock you receive when you shuffle your feet on carpet and touch a doorknob. (Yes, I've felt them!) Gates are useful—up to a point. Some dogs can climb them, while others barrel right through and knock them down.

OUTSIDE MANNERS

Does your dog tear up the yard when you're gone? Does he bark and whine until your neighbors call the police or animal control? Does he explore the neighbor's trash? Good fences make good neighbors. Your dog needs to be behind the fence and not running loose *at any time*.

Surprisingly, some people still believe that their dog should be allowed off leash to do whatever he wants. Loose dogs are a nuisance and are illegal in many areas. Most municipalities have leash laws requiring dogs to be behind a fence, in your house or on a leash. A loose dog is more apt to be hit by a car, be poisoned by unscrupulous people, get into trouble or get totally lost. Look around at your neighborhood— would you turn a five-year-old child loose, totally unsupervised, into the street to play? That's what you're doing when you turn loose a dog.

"Oh, he just hangs around home while I'm gone," you say? Want to bet? Dogs are remarkable observers and know when their owners leave and when they come home from work. You leave the house with Rover sitting on the front porch. You work for eight hours. You come home and Rover is sitting on the front porch. Do you *really* think Rover hangs out on the porch for eight hours? Ask your neighbors what he's really doing.

Okay, so the best place for your dog is behind a fence. What then? Your dog barks incessantly while you're gone. Really? What do you expect? You've left your dog alone and bored in the backyard. He'll sleep for a while, sure. But then the meter reader comes by or the letter carrier—and guess what? He barks! Or perhaps he's bored and it's hot. So he digs a nice cooling hole to lie down in. Or maybe he's a canine version of the Army Corp of Engineers and decides a nice series of tunnels or holes might be the next landscaping project.

Keep your dog inside. It will thwart dognappers—and yes, mixed breeds *do* get stolen—and people who may try to poison your dog in your own backyard. Your neighbors won't complain about the random barking and you'll actually have a garden instead of a bomb shelter this summer.

CAR RIDES

I've known plenty of dogs who hate car rides—and little wonder! All they do is go to the veterinarian or the boarding kennel when they ride in the car. I'd hate the car if all I did was go to the doctor, wouldn't you?

My own dogs love going for car rides. They go hiking, to the park or to other fun places. They may even get a hamburger at the fast food drive-through if they're being good. (Hint: Order the hamburger plain.)

Wherever you go in the car, be sure to have some way to restrain your dog. If he's old enough and well trained enough, a car harness that hooks into the seat belt will help keep your dog from getting tossed out of the car in an accident. A plastic crate is also a good investment to keep your dog safe, and to keep him from getting underfoot.

Still, a few dogs do get carsick and dislike car rides. Talk to your veterinarian about medication—they can usually suggest an over-the-counter motion sickness medication and the correct dosage.

Never, ever allow your dog to ride in the open bed of a pickup truck. Every year, many dogs are seriously injured or killed when they fall out of truck beds. Just ask a vet and they can tell you horror stories. Your dog can't hang on if you suddenly stop or swerve. Bring your dog inside the cab or tie down a crate in the back of the truck and have him ride in that.

USEFUL COMMANDS FOR GOOD MANNERS

There are several commands not within obedience training that your dog should learn. He probably knows some of them, but they are worth teaching to ensure a well-behaved dog.

Off

The "off" command means "four paws on the floor." When your dog jumps on you, push him down and tell him "off!" Then have him sit and give him a treat for obeying. Because "off" means all paws on the floor, you can also use it when your dog has sneaked up onto the bed or another piece of restricted furniture.

It's tough, but the "off" command works!

A word of caution: Don't use the word "down" for "off." If your dog is lying down on the couch, you'll confuse him, even if you're sure he knows what you *really* meant.

Drop It or Trade

"Drop it" is a useful command that you will want to teach your dog for when he picks up something really disgusting or bad for him, or something you just don't want him to have. Most dogs seem to know that these forbidden items are icky, and the quicker they wolf them down, the better, in their opinion.

You can easily teach "drop it," unless your dog's jaws are too strong or you're afraid of getting bitten. Start when your dog has something forbidden in his mouth. Squeeze open your dog's jaws by applying gentle but consistent pressure with your fingers where the upper and lower jaws meet. When your dog opens his mouth, say, "drop it," and let the item fall from his mouth. Give him a treat for being a good dog and take the item away.

The alternate command is "trade!" With "trade!" you offer something that is better than what your dog has in his mouth. Your dog will usually drop the item for something more tasty.

You can practice "trade" easily. When your dog is chewing on a rawhide or playing with a toy, offer to "trade" with something yummy. When your dog drops the toy for your treat, take the toy and give your dog the treat at the same time.

Leave It

"Leave it!" is a command that tells your dog to leave whatever interests him alone. Usually this is something you teach during the situation, using the command and a short snap of the collar. Don't forget to praise your dog when he obeys.

Out

You can tell your dog when to go to the door to go outside by associating the word "out" with the action. When you walk your dog or let him outside in the backyard, simply say, "out!" It won't take long before he learns what "out" means.

Bed

"Bed" is another command most dogs learn by association. When you tell your dog to go to his "bed" or "crate," he learns quickly what action is indicated by the word "bed." You can easily teach your dog to go into his crate by tossing a treat into his crate and telling him "bed."

Watch Me

"Watch me!" is a great command for teaching your dog to pay attention to you. It's especially good for teaching your dog to focus during chaotic situations when you must have the dog's attention.

Practicing "watch me!" is easy and teaches your dog not to be afraid to make eye contact with you. Hold up a treat and bring it to the tip of your nose. Your dog's gaze should meet your eyes. Say "watch me!" and give him the treat when you make eye contact. As you continue to practice "watch me!" you may continue to use treats or use treats some of the time and sometimes simply praise the dog.

••

CHAPTER 12

TRAINING FOR ACTIVITIES

Perhaps basic obedience isn't enough. Maybe you think you have a canine Einstein—and what proud dog owner doesn't want to show off? Even though you have a mutt, you and your pup can earn titles through the AKC, UKC and other canine organizations.

THE CANINE GOOD CITIZEN (YES, YOUR MUTT CAN EARN AN AKC TITLE)

Until 1989, the American Kennel Club wouldn't have much to do with mixed breeds. A sad but true fact. Even today, the AKC won't allow mutts to compete in most competitive sports against registered pure-breds. But even the AKC has recognized the need to show that *all* dogs can have good manners and be well socialized. So the AKC developed the Canine Good Citizen (CGC) program. Unlike other AKC titles, the Canine Good Citizen is available to all dogs, purebred or mixed, at any age, spayed, neutered or intact. Dogs who pass the test get a nifty certificate and the right to put the letters CGC after their name.

What Is the Canine Good Citizen Test?

What exactly is the Canine Good Citizen test and why is it of interest to mutt owners? It is a series of tests in which the judge passes or fails the dog. It shows the world that you have a well-trained dog whom you're proud to have as a companion. Because your dog earns a title and a certificate, you've proven yourself a conscientious dog owner. It might not get you into the local bistro with your dog, but you'd be surprised where you can go when you have a CGC on your pet. I've taken my CGC dogs to special events inside malls, to book signings and to people's houses. People have bought expensive bottled water for my dog because she was so well-behaved.

Any dog, regardless of breed or mix of breeds, can earn her Canine Good Citizen. This is Sadie.

I can't say you'll have the same experience, but most people who have well-behaved dogs leave people with favorable impressions. Your dog must pass the following tests to earn her CGC:

1. **Accepting a friendly stranger:** The dog must show no fear when someone unknown approaches the dog's owner and talks to them.

2. **Sitting politely for petting:** The dog must accept petting by a stranger when the dog is with her owner.

3. **Appearance and grooming:** The dog must accept being brushed gently by the evaluator and allow the evaluator to pick up each foot and to examine the dog's ears. The dog is also judged on whether she is clean and well-groomed.

4. **Walking on a loose lead:** The dog must walk on a loose leash and walk with her handler, including on turns and stops.

5. **Walking through a crowd:** The dog must walk through a crowd of people without pulling, jumping on people or acting fearful.

6. **Sit and down on command, and staying in place:** The dog must sit and lie down on command. The dog must then stay in place while the owner walks 20 feet away and returns to the dog. The dog may change position, but must stay in the same place.

7. **Coming when called:** The dog must wait while the owner walks 10 feet away and then calls the dog. The dog must come to the owner when called.

8. **Reaction to another dog:** The dog must show no more than a casual interest in another dog as that dog and her handler approach the first dog and her owner.

9. **Reaction to distraction:** The dog must show no fear when faced with two everyday distractions. The dog may show curiosity, but not aggression or shyness.

10. **Supervised separation:** The dog must calmly accept being left with the evaluator for three minutes while the owner is out of sight.

Training for the Canine Good Citizen Test

How do you train for the Canine Good Citizen test? As you can see from the list, the CGC test is a basic temperament and obedience test. Your dog should learn the basic obedience commands described in Chapter 10. Usually a good obedience class will help your dog prepare for the obedience portion and some of the socialization portion of the test. In obedience class, your dog will encounter other dogs and people in a controlled environment. But when the class is finished, your dog may or may not have had enough exposure for the CGC test; it really depends on the class.

You can prepare for the temperament tests by socializing your dog. Socialization starts as a puppy. Your puppy is ready to meet the world after she has had her last series of vaccinations—usually after 16 weeks. If you have adopted your dog as an adult, you can still socialize her. You'll need to make an extra effort to make up for lost time. Bring your dog to different places and allow her to greet strangers. Training classes, fun matches and dog parks are great places to socialize your dog.

If your friends are dog people, have them join you for a walk in a park or another public place where your dog is allowed. Make the experience a positive one for your dog; your friend may bring dog cookies or other treats. If, at any time, your dog becomes fearful or shy, reduce the contact a bit until she is more comfortable. For example, if your dog is shy when your friends or strangers try to pet her, don't insist on it. Instead, walk your dog on leash with your friends nearby or ask just one person to pet her.

Training for Accepting a Friendly Stranger

Most of the CGC tests require your dog to react calmly when meeting strangers or dealing with new or unexpected situations. Many dog bites occur because the dog becomes fearful in what we would consider normal situations. But these situations are far from normal if your dog has never seen them before.

Your dog should be used to someone greeting you. If she is not, bring her to places where you and she can meet people. Some owners like to bring their dogs to pet supply stores or stand in front of grocery stores where your dog can see different people. Acting calm and giving her treats for good behavior will help socialize her.

To train for the test, have a friend whom your dog does not know walk up and greet you with a handshake. You dog should not be overly excited or fearful. If your dog is excited, calm her down and put her in a sit-stay or down-stay before proceeding. Once the exercise is completed, give your dog a treat for good behavior.

Training for Sitting Politely for Petting

In this exercise, your dog will have to sit and then allow a stranger to pet her. After you practice the previous exercise, sit your dog and allow the person to pet your dog. Offer your dog treats as the person pets her, which reinforces the idea that petting by a friendly stranger is a good thing. Treats provide a distraction if your dog becomes nervous or fearful. If your dog is excited and jumps up, put her in a sit-stay and then let the person calmly pet her.

Training for Appearance and Grooming

The next exercise will demonstrate that your dog will allow a stranger to brush and comb her. Grooming and appearance make an impression on the public; if your dog is pretty, people are likely to come away with a more favorable impression than if your dog is stinky or matted. There's no reason in the world that a mutt should not be as beautiful as a Poodle or an Afghan Hound. And anyway, good grooming is essential to good health for all dogs.

If your dog hates being groomed, now is the time to teach her that grooming is fun. Okay, maybe not fun. Maybe tolerable. Start by spending five minutes a day brushing her coat. Then, pick up each foot and examine it. Most dogs hate having their feet handled, so if your dog pulls her feet away, don't hold on. Instead, try touching her feet while she has them on the floor. Slowly work toward picking up just one foot and setting it down. Then do the same for each foot.

When you've got the foot thing down, gently examine your dog's ears. Don't stick a finger in her ear canals—just touch the outside of the ear flap (the pinna) and look.

As your dog becomes used to these sessions, increase the amount of time you handle each part of the dog. Then have a friend try picking up her feet and touching her ears. If, for any reason, she pulls away, start slowly with your friend just touching her toes and the tips of her ears. Build up to where she can tolerate being touched and groomed by a stranger.

Training for Walking on a Loose Lead

Once you've finished the grooming and appearance test, you will have to demonstrate to the examiner that your dog will walk on a loose leash. She doesn't need to heel, but she does need to walk nicely on leash, without pulling. Training your dog to walk nicely on a leash is explained in Chapter 10.

Training for Walking Through a Crowd

Walking through a crowd is a bit like walking on a loose leash, but your dog will have to show the examiner that she will be polite as she walks past people. The best way to teach your dog to walk through a crowd is to walk your dog in parks and in places frequented by people. As your dog becomes accustomed to walking in places with other people and dogs, go to increasingly more crowded places. Fun matches and other events that have large numbers of people are perfect for training your dog. If your dog seems nervous at any time, give her a command (such as "watch me") to distract her from the crowds around her.

Training for Sit and Down, Stay and Come

Once you've finished walking through a crowd, you will have to demonstrate to the examiner that your dog will sit, lie down and stay. These are all basic obedience commands found in Chapter 10.

The next test is to that show your dog will come when called, and that is also covered in Chapter 10.

Training for Reaction to Another Dog

After you demonstrate that your dog will come when called, the next test is to see how your dog behaves around other dogs. If your dog is normally friendly with other dogs, this test should be relatively easy. However, if your dog is aggressive with other dogs, consult a professional trainer or behaviorist concerning your dog's aggressive behavior.

Have someone who has a dog who is friendly and not very interested in your dog train with you. Have your dogs on leash and stand about 20 feet away from each other. Tell your dog to sit and keep her focused on you with treats. Then tell your dog to heel, you and your friend will walk toward each other with your respective dogs, keeping your dogs in a close heel position as you walk. You should be a few feet apart as you pass.

Be ready to correct your dog if she shows interest in the other dog. Use the words, "No, leave it!" if your dog starts to sniff or head toward the other dog.

Stop the exercise immediately and tell both dogs to sit or lie down if either dog lunges, growls or shows aggression. Once your dogs are calm, use food as a distraction. Give the dogs some space so that neither can reach the other if one lunged. Now, start the walking exercise again. Keep your dog in the heel position and be prepared to tighten your grip the moment you see any sign of aggression. Correct the aggression and focus your dog's attention on a treat.

Training for Reaction to Distractions

After your dog has shown that she is good with other dogs, she must demonstrate that loud noises or unusual things will not bother her. The CGC test suggests such distractions as rolling a dog crate nearby, having a jogger pass by or dropping items such as a chair or a cane. The dog may certainly show a mild reaction, but she should not be fearful or shy.

If your dog has already experienced these distractions, she is less likely to react fearfully to them. Put your dog in a sit-stay and have a friend drop things or jog by. If your dog acts fearful of things your friend drops, bring her up to the items, touch them yourself and show them to her. She'll learn that they're no big deal and there isn't any cause for alarm.

Training for Supervised Separation

The last test is supervised separation. In this test, you hand your dog's leash to someone while you leave. You then go out of sight for a few minutes, and then return. While your dog may look concerned, she shouldn't whine or cry, or pull to go after you.

Training for supervised separation takes time. Most dogs who do well are used to people and activities. To train for supervised separation, start at home or someplace familiar, with your dog on a leash. Hand the leash to a friend and leave for a few moments, but remain within sight of your dog. Return to your dog, but do not make a fuss over her. Do this a few times so that she learns that even though you've handed her off to a stranger, you are returning. Repeat every day for a week, so that your dog learns that this is normal.

Next, lengthen the amount of time you're gone. Vary the time so that your dog does not know when exactly you will return. You will want to do this all within sight of your dog. Return to your dog *before* she becomes anxious or nervous. Do this for about a week with different people, so that your dog does not become accustomed to just one person.

Now your dog is ready for you to really leave, and go out of sight. Stay in sight for a little while, then "disappear." Return in sight again after a few seconds and then disappear again. Then return to your dog. In this way, your dog learns that you can disappear for a while and still return. Practice this during the week with different people. Vary the amount of time you disappear, gradually lengthening it.

Now it's time to leave out of sight and then return. Start by leaving and going out of sight for half of the longest time you disappeared in previous exercises. Practice this a few times every day, gradually lengthening the amount of time your dog must wait. Increase the time until your dog is waiting for you longer than three minutes.

Taking the Canine Good Citizen Test

Your dog is ready to take the CGC test, but where? Some obedience trainers offer CGC tests for a nominal fee. At some conformation and obedience fun matches, clubs will offer CGC testing. If you can't find a CGC tester in your area, you can go to AKC's CGC Web site at www.akc.org/love/cgc/index.cfm for a list of CGC evaluators in your area.

AGILITY (MUTTS WELCOME)

Agility is one of the fastest-growing dog sports in the world. The UKC, NADAC, USDAA and ASCA are among the organizations that allow mutts to compete in agility. You'll find contact information for these groups (and for all the sports mentioned in this chapter) in Appendix A.

STABLER

Mutts like Robyn excel in agility.

What is agility? It's a fast-paced sport where dogs go over, under, and through obstacles on a set course. They are timed, and lose points for missing obstacles or handling them incorrectly. Dogs compete both to qualify and to place.

What's so great about agility? First of all, the dogs love it. They think agility is *their* idea, not yours, once they get used to the new sport. Where else can you jump over things, climb through tunnels and stand on tables and be praised for it? Plus the treats!

Second, it gives you something fun to do with your dog. You don't need to have the fastest or most obedient dog to have fun. Your dog doesn't care if she missed an obstacle. She still had fun, and you should too.

What sort of training does your dog need to get started training in agility? Some basic obedience helps. But you don't need a perfectly trained obedience dog, just one who knows sit, lie down and stay, and will come when you call.

Obstacle Training

There are two parts to agility training: obstacle training and handling. Obstacle training teaches your dog to negotiate the obstacles correctly. This takes time. After all, these are new and exciting things for your dog to do, and not all are intuitive to her—even if they are intuitive to you. Some obstacles have moving parts, such as the seesaw, the sway bridge and the swing plank. ("Oh no! It's moving; I'd better get off!") Others, like the closed tunnel, are scary for dogs if they don't see any way out. ("I'm not going in there!") Other obstacles, like the platform jump and the weave poles, aren't intuitive to a dog at all. ("You want me to do what?")

Most obstacles have a contact area, which is a marked area your dog must step on as she gets on or off the obstacle. Contact areas are marked for the dog's safety, and you lose points if she misses them.

The obstacles vary from organization to organization. UKC has the most variety in obstacles, and focuses on control rather than speed. USDAA puts more emphasis on speed.

The obstacles include:

- **A-frame:** A contact obstacle, the A-frame is two six- to nine-foot ramps that meet in a peak at the center and are three to four feet wide. Your dog must climb the A-frame to the peak and then climb down it, touching the contact area on the way down. (NADAC, UKC, USDAA)

- **Closed tunnel:** The closed tunnel has an opening at one end (usually a barrel) with an eight- to 12-foot-long chute made of silk or parachute cloth that lies flat at the other end. Your dog will have to enter the open side of the tunnel and push her way through the chute to complete the obstacle. (NADAC, UKC, USDAA)

- **Crawl tunnel:** The dog must go underneath this long, odd-looking tunnel. It's made of PVC pipe with an adjustable cloth "ceiling." (UKC)

- **Dogwalk:** The dogwalk is a single plank connected by two elevated ramps. It is a tall obstacle, similar to a catwalk. Your dog must climb up the dogwalk, cross the plank and descend the ramp, touching contact areas on both sides. (NADAC, UKC, USDAA)

- **Hoop tunnel:** Another type of tunnel, this one is made from hoops so the dog can see all the way through. (UKC)

- **Hurdles or jumps:** There are a variety of jumps, with or without side wings, that your dog may have to jump. In AKC, UKC and USDAA, there are also low spread jumps that your dog has to clear. (NADAC, UKC, USDAA)

- **Pause box:** The pause box is entered from one side, and the dog must sit or lie down for five seconds and then leave the box. (UKC)

- **Pause table:** Although the dog steps on the table, it isn't considered a true contact obstacle. It is a square table that looks like a large end table, and can be set to various heights. Your dog must hop on the table and sit or lie down. (NADAC, UKC, USDAA)

- **Pipe tunnel or open tunnel:** The pipe tunnel can snake into various patterns, while the open tunnel is long and straight. Most dogs love tunnels. (NADAC, UKC, USDAA)

- **Seesaw:** The seesaw looks like a playground teeter-totter without the handlebars. Your dog gets on the seesaw on the downside, crosses the seesaw and tips the plank. Your dog must touch the contact zones on both sides. (NADAC, UKC, USDAA)

- **Sway bridge:** This looks like a small suspension bridge. When the dog is crossing, it does sway quite a bit. (UKC)

- **Swing plank:** This plank is suspended at four corners and moves when the dog steps on it. The dog must cross the plank, putting all four feet on it. (UKC)

- **Tire jump:** This is a jump in the shape of a tire. The tire is difficult for dogs because they must jump through instead of over. (NADAC, UKC, USDAA)

- **Weave poles:** Weave poles are six to 12 one-inch PVC pipe poles set up in a straight line anywhere from 18 to 25 inches apart. Your dog must weave through them, left, right, left, right . . . hence the name. (UKC, USDAA, NADAC)

Handling

Because all agility courses are not exactly the same, you run the course with your dog and tell her what to do, when. So once your dog learns the basics of negotiating the obstacles, *you* must then learn the basics of handling your dog and directing her over the obstacles. This isn't as easy as it sounds, and many a novice owner and dog are embarrassed at their first trial when they realize how much more they and their dog need to learn. You must learn how to send your dog over an obstacle, call your dog back from taking the wrong obstacle, and yes, teach your dog right and left.

*Robyn, a Cocker Spaniel-Golden Retriever
mix, jumps through the tire.*

Can you do this on your own? I suppose, but it would be very expensive to make or buy all the equipment. Then you would need to learn the basics of handling your dog. You could learn it from a book (and I have listed some in Appendix B), but a better solution would be to take classes from an experienced agility instructor.

Finding an Agility Training Center

Agility is a very popular dog sport, so if you live near a city or town, chances are there are agility clubs and trainers in your area. Contact local obedience clubs or training facilities in your area to find out where you and your dog can train in agility. If you can't find a club or training facility, contact the national agility organizations or surf on over to www.dogpatch.org and check out their agility calendar. Matches and trials have contact names of the trial secretary, and you should be able to locate a club or facility by asking them.

FLYBALL (NO DISCRIMINATION)

Flyball is a fast, competitive relay race where teams of four handlers and dogs compete against each other to see which team is fastest. Each dog must jump over four hurdles to a flyball box, trigger the ball by pressing a lever, catch the ball and then return over the same hurdles to the finish line—when the next dog goes. Teams that complete the relay in under 32 seconds earn points.

The North American Flyball Association (NAFA) sanctions flyball trials and awards titles to flyball participants (check out Appendix A for contact information). Any healthy dog can compete in flyball. Dogs obtain titles based on the number of points they earn.

The height of the flyball hurdles depends on the smallest team member. The hurdles are set four inches shorter than the smallest dog on the team (with a minimum of eight inches and a maximum of 16 inches), so dogs 12 inches and under are usually welcome additions to flyball teams.

Flyball requires a flyball box. Plans are available in flyball books and on the Internet, or you may buy a flyball box from an obedience supplier. You will also need four specially constructed flyball hurdles and plenty of tennis balls.

Most dogs who love to fetch also love flyball. You first train your dog to catch tennis balls as you throw them up in the air. Then you change to the flyball box, but you press the lever. Eventually, you teach your dog to trigger the mechanism. Some dogs become so proficient at knowing when the ball is ready to come out that they have their mouth open and waiting before it pops out!

Robyn again, showing her versatility in flyball.

FLYING DISC (MUTTS MAKE FANTASTIC DISC DOGS)

Playing with a flying disc is so much more fun when your dog joins the game. Any healthy dog with sound structure can become a flying disc dog. Not surprisingly, the best disc dogs are mutts, not purebreds. Even if you decide not to compete, flying disc is a great way to exercise your dog.

If your dog knows how to play fetch, the flying disc shouldn't be too difficult to teach. Many people start by making the flying disc a desirable object for their dog. Feed your dog from the flying disc, roll it along the ground on its side so your dog will chase the disc, and reward your dog every time she plays with or picks up the flying disc. Some people use specially made discs designed for dogs during training, which add to the interest, since they are meat-scented. Whichever disc you use, be certain it is soft and flexible. The hard, inflexible discs can hurt when caught in a dog's mouth, and may break teeth.

FREESTYLE DANCING (PUTTIN' ON THE RITZ)

A great new sport has opened up for dogs of all breeds and all mixes. In freestyle, you choreograph a dance routine for you and your dog to perform together, to music. More than just heeling to music, freestyle incorporates a variety of subtle and intricate moves. Creativity is paramount. It's fun and challenging for both you and your dog.

Freestyle is a relatively new sport, appearing in the 1990s. Officially, the World Canine Freestyle Organization (WCFO) was founded in June 1999 after some evolutionary changes from another freestyle organization. Another organization, Canine Freestyle Federation (CFF), holds freestyle events as well.

Freestyle has two basic formats: heelwork to music and musical freestyle. Each format may be split into classes: Juniors, Singles, Pairs and Teams.

Heelwork to music requires that the dog stay within four feet of the handler at all times. The dog may not perform any distance work, such as jumps, weaves, send outs, distance spins and pivots. Props are allowed, provided they are part of the routine in some fashion. Training collars of any type, other than a standard slip collar, are not allowed in the ring, nor are training aids (food, toys, etc.).

Musical freestyle has fewer rules than heelwork to music. Any move, provided it is not dangerous, may be used. Innovation and creativity are the keys here. Props are allowed, provided they are part of the routine in some fashion. But again, training collars and aids are not.

THERAPY DOGS (LOVE KNOWS NO BREED)

Is your dog a cuddler? Does she love to meet people and snuggle with them? Maybe she can brighten a patient's day at a local hospital or nursing home. Therapy dogs provide positive interaction for people at various care facilities. Dogs are wonderful for helping patients become less withdrawn and happier.

A therapy dog must have good manners and general obedience training, and be neat and well-groomed. Your dog must like having strangers pet her and should be calm in strange situations. Usually passing some type of temperament test, such as the AKC CGC test, is required by therapy dog training organizations.

How do you get involved in therapy dog training? Contact local hospitals and nursing home facilities to find out who runs their therapy dog program and get in contact with that person. Or contact the Delta Society or Therapy Dogs International for more information (both are listed in Appendix A).

• •

MESSED-UP MUTTS

As much as we love our dogs and think of them as kids, sometimes we end up with a problem child. If you adopted your mutt as an adult, you might have discovered he picked up a bad habit or two before he came to live with you. Or your dog may have developed a bad habit in response to his new situation. Regardless of whether you or someone else caused your dog's behavior problem, it's now up to you to fix it.

PROBLEM CHILD

Don't think for a moment that someone else will fix your dog's problem. The shelters are full of pets who have behavioral problems—most are put down because their owners didn't care enough to try to fix them. Instead of handing your dog off to someone else or condemning him to a terrifying return to a shelter, identify the cause of the problem and fix it.

Sometimes these problems manifest themselves slowly. Other times, you see just the problem but no apparent cause. How do you determine the cause of the behavior?

Biological Causes

Before assuming that your dog's bad behavior is behavioral, make sure it is not biological. A dog in pain can become irritable and grumpy. Hip dysplasia, arthritis and other joint problems can be very painful, and dogs with these conditions hate being touched. I had one female who was aggressive toward other females until she was spayed—her hormones were literally driving her crazy. I had a sled dog who quit on me because of a hidden heart condition that manifested itself later in life. (I retired him early, thinking he just didn't like to run in a sled team.) Another female I knew was very nasty toward other dogs but actually had hip dysplasia. Urinary tract infections can cause incontinence. Thyroid problems, which are not uncommon in dogs, can cause behavior changes. Likewise, some medications can cause what appear to be behavioral problems.

If the problem appears out of nowhere—or even if it doesn't—take your dog for a thorough health check. Talk with your veterinarian about the problem and see if they can find a root cause for the bad behavior. Sometimes they can; sometimes they can't. Even if your vet rules out a biological component, keep it in mind in case the condition is subtle and your vet may have missed it.

Trouble on the Horizon

Problems often start innocently enough. Most dog owners are unaware that certain behaviors can lead to a problem: a low growl when your kid walks by your dog when the dog is eating, or maybe he lifted his leg once in the house. Maybe you left some chicken wings out and your dog has filched them, or maybe you've caught him up on the couch. Or maybe someone left the gate open once and now your dog is digging around the fence.

You might explain the behavior away ("He was protecting his food" or "He loves chicken"), or you might ignore it and hope it was a one-time thing. Maybe it wasn't that big of a problem ("I can clean that up" or "I really don't care if he sleeps there"), but it's a problem that can quickly get out of hand. Soon, the problem becomes big ("He's always lifting his leg on things" or "He snapped at me"). Before you know it, you have a problem child.

What You Do to Encourage Bad Behavior

As I've implied above, the owner is largely responsible for allowing bad behavior to continue. For example, your puppy is nippy and you allow him to chew on your hands instead of teaching him "no bite." The puppy grows bigger and bites harder; his sharp teeth start hurting and piercing your skin. At this point you want to stop the behavior, but now he finds your efforts funny or annoying. The behavior is now a habit.

It is better to stop a bad habit when it first starts—or better yet, prevent the behavior altogether. Look at what entices your dog: food on the counter, a weak fence, the trash bin left out. If you take the things away that tempt your dog, he won't behave badly. After all, your dog can't raid the garbage if he can't get to it. Nor can he annoy the neighbors with his barking if he's inside at night or in the daytime when you're gone.

Fixing Ingrained Bad Habits

While it's always preferable to stop bad habits before they start, if you get an older dog he may have learned some bad habits in his other home. These bad habits might have contributed to him being up for adoption (or out on the street) it the first place.

When faced with a new situation (such as a new home), most dogs won't show their bad habits until they get comfortable in their new surroundings. Because he can't tell you what he's done in his other home, your dog's antics might surprise you. Then again, he may show no bad habits because the stimulus isn't there (for example, you keep the trash locked away or you don't leave him out all night to bark).

Once you see a bad behavior (counter raiding, digging, excessive barking and so on), you now must assume your dog has done this in the past. Fix the problem *now*. That means if he's a counter raider, keep all foodstuffs out of your dog's reach (in the refrigerator, in an oven or in a cabinet), or crate him when the food is out. If you like having your dog out while you eat, you or someone else in your family will have to watch him closely to be sure that he doesn't snatch the food while you're not looking. It takes only once and the behavior is rewarded.

AGGRESSION

Aggression is a serious problem and should not be ignored. Different types of aggression have different causes; once you understand your dog's aggression, you can work to correct it. I'm not talking about an occasional growl or maybe a dogfight between canine buddies where the play turns a little nasty. I'm talking aggression; where the dog is consistently aggressive toward other dogs or people.

Some types of aggression have biological causes. Pain, seizures and other medical conditions can cause a dog to show aggression. Some deadly diseases such as rabies can cause aggression. If your dog shows aggression, you should first take him to a veterinarian to determine if the condition is medical. If not, take your dog to an experienced trainer or animal behaviorist who has had success in working with aggressive dogs.

Make no mistake: In this litigious society, an aggressive dog is a liability. If you own a dog with an aggression problem, you *must* correct it. Otherwise, someone or someone's dog may be seriously injured or even killed.

Aggression types such as pain aggression or fear aggression are understandable, and the behavior clearly emerges under duress. Other types of aggression may not be so easy to deal with. But deal with them you must. And you must work with a professional on this.

Here are some of the types of aggression you may see in dogs:

- **Prey aggression:** In a number of breeds and mixes, the dog mistakes another animal as a prey item (dinner on the run) and chases it. The dog usually will not back down because he sees the object of his aggression as food. This behavior has been modified in herding dogs, where the dog exhibits all the behaviors of prey aggression, but doesn't attack the animal.

- **Dominance aggression:** The dog shows aggression because he decides other people or animals have intruded upon his authority. The dog may not back down with this type of aggression.

- **Fear aggression:** The dog is frightened by something and is trying to get away. Usually it's a few quick snaps or a bite, and then the dog retreats.

- **Pain aggression:** The dog is in pain and bites because he thinks he has to protect himself. Like fear aggression, it is usually a few quick bites and the dog retreats.

- **Guarding or territorial aggression:** The dog is trying to prevent someone from taking away something of his or from entering his territory. Usually he doesn't pursue the intruder once the intruder leaves.

- **Frustration or redirected aggression:** The dog bites because of frustration or because he can't get at something his aggression is focused on. He may snap or bite once or twice. If the frustration is redirected, it can take the form of any of the other types of aggression.

- **Sexual aggression:** The dog is competing for a mate. Once other suitors are driven off, the dog isn't concerned with them.

- **Idiopathic aggression:** This is usually biological and has no apparent triggers. The dog attacks without any provocation or signal. It may be a quick growl and snap, all the way up to a full-on attack. Usually it's seizure-like aggression—the dog appears to be unaware he is doing it at all.

Some dogs will show a mixture of these types of aggression. For example, a dog showing dominance aggression may also show guarding and prey aggression.

The best way to stop aggressive tendencies is proper training and socialization. Spaying and neutering will help reduce hormone-caused aggression due to sexual urges and dominance behavior. Teaching your dog to trade for items and teaching him that he mustn't guard his toys or food will help eliminate guarding aggression. Keep your dog away from other aggressive dogs to prevent him from learning to be aggressive toward other dogs.

EXCESSIVE BARKING

Most dogs bark. Some dogs emit other vocalizations instead of barking, but most make some sort of noise. Dogs bark for a variety of reasons. Or they bark for no reason. They need to bark and you cannot—and should not—try to prevent a dog from barking altogether. But too much barking will get you in trouble with the local animal control and local ordinances.

Dogs are often encouraged to bark from the beginning. The dog sees someone down the street and barks. His owner says, "Oh what a good dog!" and Rover gets rewarded. Or maybe the owner doesn't praise him, but the person sees Rover and acts fearful. Rover thinks, "I'm big and tough now—I'll bark!" Either way, the barking is reinforced.

Rover quickly becomes an idiot barker. He barks at the squirrels. He barks at the leaves blowing in the wind. He barks at the moon. You've seen Rover, haven't you? He just likes barking. He's like someone who talks too much—they like hearing the sound of their own voice.

Assuming you weren't the cause of your dog's barking—and even if you were—how do you shut him up? First of all, you shouldn't be leaving him outside all day while you're gone or all night while you sleep. (And trust me, owners of big-mouth dogs can sleep through anything, including their barking!) Keep him inside. Your neighbors will thank you.

But suppose he's barking indoors or barking outside when you're home? You can take several empty soda cans and put a few pennies in them. Squish the can or tape the top closed so that it holds the pennies and rattles. When your dog is barking, hurl a can in his direction. (Don't hit him!) The rattle should make enough noise to startle him and he will fall silent. If you do it right, it'll be discipline from God, not from you. When he barks again, hurl another can. Eventually, he'll decide that's not really what he wants to happen. You can also use a squirt gun or squirt bottle. Get one of those super soakers if your dog is large or if your yard is big. A blast from a squirt gun usually silences a dog.

What if your dog barks or whines inside and you have an apartment? You can buy a citronella collar that is activated by barking. In the collar is a tiny canister of citronella spray that sprays under the chin when the dog barks. Citronella is a strong scent and most dogs hate it. A couple of whiffs and your dog will associate barking with getting sprayed under the chin.

CHEWING

All dogs love to chew. It's natural for them. That means they must have appropriate chew toys. But when they chew your things instead, that's a problem. If your dog is chewing inappropriate items, ask yourself when your dog is chewing them. Did you leave him alone at home, loose and able to chew up any item he can get in his mouth? Is he sneaking into another room while you're in the kitchen? Once you pinpoint the behavior, you can work on a solution.

If your dog is normally an angel and has turned into a chewing fiend, you may wish to have your vet examine him. Tooth, mouth and digestive problems can all cause excessive chewing. Puppies who are teething will also chew until their new teeth come in and their old teeth come out. Sometimes a puppy tooth will not fall out and will become inflamed, causing pain. Your vet may have to extract it.

If you've determined that the chewing behavior is not related to biological problems, your next step is to stop the chewing. That means any time you can't watch your dog, he needs to be in his crate—with an appropriate chew toy. That includes when you're out of the house or asleep. You can't expect to give your dog full run of the house unsupervised. It's like inviting a group of teenagers to your home and having an open keg of beer: an invitation for disaster.

But suppose he sneaks off to chew things? Try tethering him to you (see the box on page 120). He'll be forced to follow you around and pay attention to you—and won't be able to sneak off and chew something. While he is sitting around, give him something appropriate to chew. If he chews something inappropriate, offer to trade with an appropriate item. Correct him with a "no!" and give him the correct item to chew instead.

Putting things your dog likes to chew out of reach is a good idea. But if you can't (maybe he likes to chew the table leg), try making the items less palatable. You can use bitter agents, such as Bitter Apple spray, on inappropriate items that your dog normally chews.

How long does it take before your dog becomes completely reliable? Some unlearn this bad habit in a month or two, but many take longer. Some can never be trustworthy or may only be trustworthy while you're around. But by preventing the destructive behavior or eliminating the temptation, you should be able to reduce the amount of destructiveness.

JUMPING UP

Your dog may be enthusiastic when he greets you, but jumping up isn't appropriate. Your dog can ruin your good clothes, knock over your guests or injure a child or an older person.

An old trick was to put your knee up when a dog jumped. The problem with this tactic is that quite often the dog simply bounces off and jumps again. A better solution is to teach your dog to sit when he is greeting people. When your dog jumps up, tell him, "No! Off!" and put his feet on the ground. ("Off" is the command for four paws on the ground, remember?) Then tell him to sit. Don't pet him until he sits. Then praise him quietly, "Good dog, what a good dog." If he jumps up, stop petting and put him in a sit.

If you are consistent with this training, he will eventually learn that to receive petting, he must sit nicely for people.

FEAR OF THUNDER OR LOUD NOISES

Dogs who are afraid of thunder may have been encouraged by their former owners if they were coddled during thunderstorms ("oh poor thing!"), or may simply be afraid. Although it's not a scientific observation, I've noticed that most dogs who are afraid of thunder or loud noises are born this way, and the problem actually becomes worse with age. Again, it's not a scientific observation, but shepherds and shepherd mixes seem to have a worse time with thunder than dogs with other breeds in them.

It's not easy to correct this problem with training or desensitization. The best thing is to crate your dog during thunderstorms or times when there are fireworks, such as Fourth of July and New Year's Eve. Put him in a safe environment where he can't accidentally hurt himself or escape. Some medications are available from your veterinarian that might help lessen his panic.

HOUSE SOILING

If your dog has never been reliably housetrained, start by housetraining him (as explained in Chapter 7). Put him on a schedule and have him in a crate or on a tether (see the box below). However, if he has suddenly started eliminating in the house, you may have another problem.

First, be certain there aren't any medical conditions or medications that may be causing a lapse in housetraining. Your veterinarian will be able to determine this. If you've determined that your dog has a behavioral problem, start housetraining from scratch, but with one important exception: Establish yourself as alpha (see Chapter 9) to be sure there are no dominance issues at work. If your dog decides to sneak off and piddle while you're not looking, try tethering him to you.

HOUDINI DOG

Houdini dogs are really smart. More clever than the average house mutt, Houdinis find challenge in steel bars and diabolical fences. If you watch the Houdini dog at work, you'll actually see him study the layout of a pen or fence to see if there is some way he can outwit it.

These clever canine fellows are made, not born, but there appears to be a tendency to escape in certain breeds. Usually clever hound mixes and Northern breed mixes will be more inclined to be escape artists, but *any* dog is capable. Owners create Houdini dogs by giving them inferior barriers. The dog figures out how to get out and the owner puts up a slightly stronger barrier. The dog soon learns that with a little extra effort, he can still get out. And so it continues.

TETHERING

I first learned about tethering nearly 20 years ago with my first dog, Conan, who had a bit of a housebreaking issue. Some trainers also call it "umbilical cording." The idea is, whenever your dog is out of the crate, he must be attached to you with a long line. Wherever you go, he goes. It forces the dog to focus on you instead of on what he wants to do.

The tethering also helps keep your dog from sneaking out of the room and doing naughty things, like marking or defecating or chewing things up.

How do you stop the Houdini dog? Well, if yours is just starting, you're in luck! Put up fencing that he can't dig under, climb over or jump over. Keep him crated inside when you're gone. You can stop the Houdini in his tracks.

What if your dog is an adult Houdini? Think POW: How is he going to break out of this? Look at your fence and your yard. You may have to build a special kennel with a roof so he can't climb out. You may have to clip or tie the latch on the gate so he can't undo it. You must watch the adult Houdini constantly. Otherwise, he'll be rewarded with his escape. Eventually, once he learns he can't escape, he might give up.

Regardless of which type of Houdini you have, exercise (both mental and physical) will go a long way to preventing escapes. Bored dogs become Houdinis; tired dogs have no energy to escape.

RAIDING PARTIES

Some dogs love raiding counters, tables and trash for tidbits. Some are sneaky and some are brash, but regardless of the method, this is a tough habit to break. If your dog gets away with it once, all the scolding in the world won't matter because your dog has hit the jackpot, and there's a food reward every time he succeeds.

Start by assessing what you keep on your counters and where you keep your trash. Keep the trash behind closed doors where your dog can't get to it, and keep food in cabinets with childproof latches (available at any hardware store). If your dog has learned to open the refrigerator (don't laugh—some mutts are quite capable!), there are childproof straps for them as well.

Keep your food out of reach when it's unattended. Many people find their conventional and microwave ovens to be a safe haven for dinner plates. If you have a confirmed counter raider and have to have a lot of food out (a party, for example), you should crate your dog where he can't get into trouble.

SEPARATION ANXIETY

Some dogs become frantic when their owners leave, and turn to destructive behavior and whining as an outlet for their anxiety. Sometimes the owner causes this behavior by making a big deal out of leaving the house. They return to find their dog upset, and coddle him when they return ("Did you miss Mommy?").

Some of the destructiveness might be due to boredom and opportunity. You're gone and you've just left your entire home as your dog's playground. Crate him when you leave and don't make a big deal out of leaving or returning. This will help some forms of separation anxiety.

However, like fear of thunder and other loud noises, separation anxiety can be ingrained. First, crate your dog to be sure he can't be destructive while you're gone. If he whines or cries, a citronella bark collar may help curb his barking (see Excessive Barking). In some instances, your veterinarian may be able to help your dog's anxiety with certain medications.

DIGGING

Digging is natural for many dogs, including those with terrier and Northern breed backgrounds. Dogs dig for a number of reasons: to bury things, to unbury things, to dig cooling holes and dens, and for the sheer pleasure of digging. It's a tough habit to break.

Most dogs hate digging where their feces are buried, so backfilling the hole with your dog's feces and covering it with a layer of dirt will stop him from digging in those places. If your dog digs when you're not a home, you may have to keep him inside or put him in a dig-proof kennel run (one lined with concrete). If he digs when you're home, you can try the pennies-in-a-soda-can method or squirt-bottle method (as described in "Excessive Barking").

Some people are able to train their dog to dig in one place by rewarding and praising their dog when he digs in the right place, and correcting the dog when he digs in an inappropriate place. It's a good idea to give a digger an appropriate place to dig, rather then trying to break the habit entirely.

· ·

CHAPTER 14

ON THE ROAD AGAIN

Traveling with your pet can be a pleasure or a nightmare, depending on your planning and your pet. There are a variety of reasons to travel with your mutt: You're on vacation and you'd like to bring your dog along, you're moving to another place and you're bringing your dog along (of course!), you're on a business trip and no one's around to take care of your pet, or you're visiting friends or relatives who are dog people too. Whatever the reason, you've decided that bringing your dog along is best.

Before you start packing, start thinking. Taking a vacation with a dog requires a lot more time and preparation than taking one without the dog. You can't just jump in the car and go somewhere.

Not all pets are good travelers and many pets get carsick or behave inappropriately in new surroundings. In some cases, it's better to board your dog or hire a pet sitter than to put her through the stress of a trip.

Likewise, some places are poor choices to bring your dog. Before you decide to bring your dog with you, find out if there are places where you can take your dog and facilities such as boarding kennels and emergency veterinarians in the area you're visiting. What are you going to do while you're there? Is your dog going to be cooped up in her crate all day in the hotel room or will you be going to places where dogs are allowed?

Some dogs *shouldn't* travel unless you have no other choice. Young puppies, elderly dogs and untrained dogs should *not* join you on your vacation. Hire a pet sitter or use a boarding kennel. Basic obedience commands—sit, down, come, heel—*aren't* optional on the road, they're imperative. The only time you should transport such a dog is if you're moving. A possible alternative to riding in a car with your dog might be to ship her by airplane, but this has its own problems too. If there is no alternative, talk with your veterinarian about possible sedatives—for the dog, not you! A sedative may help ease the travel stress.

Make sure your dog is up-to-date on all her vaccinations, including rabies. If you're traveling in Lyme disease country or places where your dog might be exposed to *Giardia* (rural towns with limited water treatment facilities), ask your vet if a Lyme disease or a *Giardia* vaccine is appropriate. Also ask about heartworm preventives if your dog isn't already taking them. Your vet can also advise you on what other vaccinations or medications might be appropriate for your dog.

BEFORE YOU GO

Before you pack, before you head on out on your grand adventure, consider your dog. You will have to make reservations in hotels that allow pets. And just because the hotel allows pets doesn't mean they'll allow your dog. Sad but true—many hotels and motels have size restrictions. Some say cat and dogs under X lbs are okay—as if a larger dog might do more damage! Some will charge an extra fee to have the dog in the room. Some want a refundable deposit.

Whatever you do, don't think you can just sneak in your dog. Most motel owners are pretty savvy about what goes on. Every year, I stay at a little motel in Utah at the same time with my dogs. The last time I was there, the woman at the desk said, "Oh, you're the folks who stay every year one night." She remembered me and my dogs. Hopefully, we've made a good impression because we always try to be quiet and we always pick up after the dogs.

If you try to sneak in your dog, you might find an extra bill tagged to your room charge—or worse, find out you've been evicted. Not the kind of vacation you had in mind, was it?

Consider the type of vacation you're taking. Some places are naturally nice for dogs; others are not. Large cities with attractions where dogs aren't allowed may not be fun for your dog at all. Even some places you would think would be perfect to bring your dog may not allow dogs or may severely restrict them. National and state parks are good examples. Many do not allow dogs in the backcountry, although they will allow dogs on major logging roads and other areas. Check with the park service before discovering that your best friend isn't welcome.

You'll naturally be bringing food along, but you may want to also bring bottled water. Some dogs' stomachs and intestines are sensitive to water in other areas of the country and may have digestive upsets. In rural areas, it's a good idea to bring your own water anyway. Some places are on well water or their treatment facilities can't screen out

FINDING A PLACE THAT ALLOWS DOGS

It seems the travel industry has discovered pets. Most hotel and motel chains list whether their hotels and motels allow pets and what amenities are available for them. The AAA also lists hotels and motels and whether they allow pets. One word of caution: Don't rely solely on these lists, because policies change. Always call and ask.

Here are some useful travel guides that will help you find acommodations:

> *Pets on the Go: The Definitive Pet Accommodation and Vacation Guide,* by Dawn Habgood and Robert Habgood, Dawbert Press, 2002.

> *Traveling With Your Pet: The AAA PetBook, 5th Edition,* the Automobile Association of America, 2003.

> *Great Vacations for You and Your Dog, USA, 2003–04,* Martin Management Books, 2003.

> *Fodor's Road Guide USA: Where to Stay With Your Pet,* Fodor's Travel Publications, 2001.

> *The Portable petswelcome.com: The Complete Guide to Traveling With Your Pet,* by Fred N. Grayson and Chris Kingsley, Howell Book House, 2001.

> *Mobil 2004 Travel Guide: On the Road With Your Pet,* Fodor's Travel Publications, 2004.

microorganisms such as *Giardia* (which causes severe diarrhea and dehydration). Plan on bringing enough food and water for a day or two longer than your vacation, in case of unforeseen delays.

Health Certificates

When you travel across state lines or into another country, you'll need your pet's health certificate. You can obtain one of these certificates before you leave from your veterinarian. These usually cost no more than $25 and the certificate must be dated no earlier than 10 days from the time you travel. If you travel by plane, you must have a certificate to transport your dog.

Have copies of your dog's health certificate and vaccination certificates with you at all times. This means you should make a copy to keep with you if your dog travels by plane (the health certificate usually remains fixed to the dog's crate).

Airline Travel

Airline travel presents a whole different set of obstacles. When you're flying with a dog, be sure to contact the airline well before you buy your tickets to find out what the airline's (and the FAA's) latest rules and regulations are regarding transporting dogs. Some airlines will not transport dogs at all, while others may have size or temperature restrictions. Unless you have a very small dog, your mutt will have to go as baggage in the cargo hold.

Assuming you can fly with your dog, arrive several hours before your flight to get through security and get your dog ready to be loaded onto the airplane. The airline may require food and water dishes, but if your dog chews plastic (many do!), I've found that clipping a small stainless steel bucket (available through pet supply catalogues) with a double snap to the inside of the crate works as well as a water bowl. Prepackage some dog food and tape that to the top of the crate.

You should also have a package with all your dog's paperwork, stating where your dog is going, your home address and phone number, your cell phone number, any emergency numbers and any specific instructions, in case you get separated from her. Include copies of all health records and vaccinations. I usually include a nice note to the baggage handlers, such as: "Hi! My name is Rover and I'm an Australian Shepherd mix. I'm very important to my owner. I'm very friendly, but I'm a little nervous right now. My owner is Maggie Bonham from 12345 Street Name Way, Denver, Colorado 80123, (303) 123-4567. I'm flying UA 123 to SLC. She'll be staying at the Radisson Hotel, phone number. . . ." It's a little chatty, but it gives the baggage handlers some information and also shows that you care enough to give them instructions on how to care for your dog.

The American Veterinary Medical Association advises against sedating your dog when you fly, because the combination of high altitude and sedatives can cause problems for some dogs.

I've used several different airlines to transport dogs over the years, and each time, I've been pleased. Most are keenly aware that your dog is your baby and are willing to accommodate you. I know that there have been horror stories, but they have, thankfully, not been my experience.

Car Travel

Some dogs do remarkably well in the car. Others would rather have their nails pulled out with a pair of pliers. If your dog is used to traveling to fun places in the car, you'll have little problem getting her ready for a big trip. If your dog hates riding in the car, perhaps you should rethink bringing her along—unless you're moving. In this case, talk to your veterinarian about sedatives, and keep your dog in a crate.

When you travel by car, you should have your dog either in a crate or wearing a seat harness restraint. Either of these will minimize injury in case of an accident or if you have to stop suddenly. They're also useful for keeping your dog out of your lap while you're driving. Check on your dog frequently if you use a crate, especially in the summertime. Be sure your dog is cool and there is enough air flowing through the crate to avoid the dangers of overheating.

This brings up the subject of temperature on your trip. In warm weather, temperatures inside a car can soar to dangerous levels in a short time, even with the windows down. Be sure your car's air conditioner is in good working order and make sure the air vents around your dog's crate aren't blocked. Likewise, be sure the sun doesn't hit your dog's crate directly while you're driving. *Never leave a dog alone inside a car,* even with the windows cracked, during summer. Even in a relatively short time, the car can heat up to fatal temperatures.

One useful device is a portable fan that runs on batteries. These are great to clip onto your dog's crate, and will help keep her cool in hot weather. In very hot weather, I take two-liter plastic soda bottles, fill them with water and then freeze them. You can put one or more in your dog's crate as coolers, and as the ice melts, you can then give her the cold water to drink.

Cold weather can be also dangerous if your mutt has a single coat (terrier or Poodle-type mixes). In this case, keeping your dog warm is important. Keep her on a warm blanket. Dog coats or sweaters are not silly if your dog lacks enough fur to keep her warm.

Plan no more than four hours of driving between stops (more frequently if your dog is old or a puppy). Rest stops frequently have places to exercise your dog, but do so only on a leash. Many dogs who are normally reliable off leash may not be in unfamiliar surroundings. Be a responsible owner and pick up after your dog when she defecates.

EQUIPMENT CHECKLIST

This is the minimum checklist for traveling with your dog:

- Health certificates and vaccination certificates
- Phone numbers for emergency veterinarians in the area
- Canine first aid kit
- Enough food and water for your trip plus two days
- Travel crate
- Extra leash
- Paper towels and plastic bags
- Spot cleaner (enzymatic cleaners)
- Bags for picking up pet waste
- Treats
- Toys
- Portable cooling fans (battery powered)
- Dog's medication
- Collar with ID tags for both your destination and your home

Get Your Vehicle Checked

Surprisingly, people seldom think about their cars when they're talking about traveling with dogs. But the greatest single point of failure for a trip is your automobile. Think about how miserable it would be if you had a breakdown on the highway with your dog or if your air conditioner stopped working in the middle of Nevada in the summertime.

Be sure your vehicle is in good running order. Have it tuned up and inspected for any possible failures. Both the heater and the air conditioner should be in good working order. Have your brakes and tires checked. Are you hearing any squeaks or squeals? This could suggest a water pump, steering box or potential belt failure.

ID, Please

Before you leave on a trip, be certain your dog has two forms of ID—tags that change as you change your location, and a permanent form, either a microchip or tattoo. Tags, because not everyone knows to look for permanent ID; permanent ID, because your dog may lose her collar and tags. (See Chapter 20 for more information on identification.)

Hotels and Motels

Always show good manners with your dog whenever you travel. Sadly, many people abuse their welcome and some hotels and motels that once accepted dogs no longer do. Always be mindful of the hotel's hospitality. Here are some good rules for being a good guest:

- **Always inform the hotel or motel when you make your reservation that you have a dog.**
- **Never leave your dog alone in your room.** A crated dog may howl or bark and disturb guests. A loose dog may destroy things or soil the carpet.
- **Ask the front desk where you can exercise your dog.** Bring a plastic bag or pooper scoop and pick up all feces.
- **Don't bathe, brush or groom your dog in a hotel room.**
- **Don't let your dog sleep in the bed with you.** The next person may not like dog hair on the blankets and bedspread. If your dog can't sleep except on a bed, bring an extra blanket or towel and lay it across the bed to keep the fur off.
- **Put your dog's dishes in the bathroom or anywhere there is a tiled or linoleum floor.** Dogs sometimes spill food and water when eating or drinking.
- **Do not let your dog off leash to run.**
- **Keep your dog quiet.**
- **Use a lint brush or dog hair roller to remove any dog hair from the furniture and carpet.**
- **Leave the room in good shape.**
- **Choose a first floor room, hopefully with a door that goes outside, so you can take your dog outside quickly if she needs to eliminate.** Plus, it's easier to not have to drag her crate into an elevator.
- **Choose a hotel that offers room service so you don't have to go out to eat.**

Campgrounds

Many campgrounds allow dogs. Like hotels and motels, be sure to advise the campground caretakers that you have a dog and find out where you can exercise her. Keep your dog inside the tent or camper at night and don't allow her to run loose where she can harass wildlife and other campers.

While it's a lot of fun to run loose in the great outdoors, many dogs aren't as obedient as Robyn, especially when they're in unfamiliar surroundings. So keep your dog on a leash!

Show the same consideration with your dog as you would at a hotel or motel. Whining or barking dogs can be as big a nuisance as they would be in a hotel. Likewise, be sure to pick up after your dog—no one enjoys the great outdoors with dog poop on their shoes!

EMERGENCIES

What should you do when something unexpected happens? Maybe your dog gets injured or sick—or lost. What do you do? Don't panic. You can't fix the problem if you're panicking. Calm down and assess the situation. Then look for help.

Sick or Injured Dog

If your dog is sick or injured, you need to take her to the nearest emergency veterinarian. When I'm traveling with dogs, the Yellow Pages have worked for me. In one case, when my sled dogs were injured in a squabble, I contacted a veterinarian listed as the chief veterinarian in a sled dog race. He was able to stitch my dog up right away and prescribe antibiotics. Later, another one of my dogs had a urinary tract infection and required medication. In both instances, local people were able to direct me to the veterinarian.

But let's say you don't know anyone. Ask the front desk or the concierge at a motel or hotel. One fellow dog writer, Kim Thornton, was in Kansas City (far from home) and had to take her dog, Bella, to the vet. When she called a cab to go to a 24-hour veterinary hospital, the cab driver actually knew a closer hospital that was open and took her there. It makes sense that most cab drivers know what's open and available on their shift, so ask!

Lost Dog

A lost dog is a nightmare for anyone who has experienced it, but for someone traveling, the situation is even worse. If your dog escapes and you can no longer find her, contact the local animal control, the local police department and any veterinarians and shelters in the immediate area. Alert the hotel or motel staff where you're staying.

Some people post flyers and even post on various Internet e-mail lists about their lost dog, but their effectiveness is questionable. Many people don't read flyers tacked to signposts, and while there are plenty of good people on the Internet, a vast majority won't ever be in the place you are. The USDA has a Web site for posting lost pets to the missing pet network: www.missingpet.net.

Many stray dogs are picked up within a few hours of getting out. There are a few who manage to elude capture for more than a few days. Unless they're totally mystified by their surroundings, many dogs are able to find their way back to their owners if they're loose. If you can stay where you lost your dog for a few days, do it. You might be able to find her again when she decides she's hungry and comes looking for you.

My own nightmare came from a new dog who escaped from his kennel. Although I was barely his owner for a day, I had fed him. Later that night, he appeared looking for more food and I was able to catch him with a box of dog biscuits.

Preventing (and Preparing for) the Unthinkable

A sick, injured or lost dog can make traveling a nightmare. But it *can* happen. So prepare for the unthinkable.

Here's a checklist for preparing for and preventing emergencies:

- Know the local veterinary hospitals, veterinary emergency rooms, boarding kennels, animal control, police and other important numbers where you'll be staying.

- Always have two forms of ID (tags and a permanent form) on your dog.

- Have a full canine first-aid kit with you.

- Have a cell phone with you. It's necessary for providing a number if your dog is lost.

- Keep your dog secure at all times. Keep your dog on a leash. Make sure the hotel or motel room is shut securely before letting your dog loose in the room. When you can't watch her or be with her, put her in her crate in a secure place.

- Put your dog in a local kennel for a few days (or even a few hours) if you can't watch her. Check kennel fencing for potential escape routes.

- Know the fire escape routes in your hotel so that you aren't worrying about a panicking dog *and* how to get out.

• •

CHAPTER 15

FOOD FOR THOUGHT

Open a bag of dog food and pour it in a bowl. What could be easier? But how do you know your mutt is getting the right nutrition? Why are you feeding that dog food to Rover? Is it because you recognize the brand? Is it because it was on sale? Did your vet recommend it? Did the person at the pet supply store recommend it?

Maybe you're not feeding a commercial dog food. Maybe you heard that the ingredients in pet foods cause cancer or they're not complete and balanced or your dog just doesn't like dog food. Maybe someone told you that you can feed him fresh fruits and vegetables and raw meat and bones, and give your dog a balanced diet that way. Or maybe you're just feeding him table scraps.

You may be feeding your mutt a balanced diet or you may be feeding him something less than optimal. In many cases, well-meaning people may be giving you bad advice. Not all dog foods are the same, and in most cases, homemade diets fall seriously short of providing adequate nutrition. Just as you wouldn't expect a car to run on kerosene, you can't expect a dog to remain healthy without the right fuel.

CHOOSING YOUR DOG'S FOOD

If you're not already feeding your dog a premium dog food, start now. You want premium brands because of the quality of ingredients. Generic and bargain brand dog foods are chock-full of fillers that your dog doesn't need. The protein sources in premium dog foods are highly digestible, meaning that your dog can use more of the protein. As a result, you feed less and have less dog waste to pick up.

Why are premium dog foods so much more expensive than the generic brands? Because of the quality of the ingredients. But because they also have more nutrition, you feed less than a generic brand, so you

Feed your dog the best possible nutrition. It will make a huge difference in his health and in his life. This is Skye, the author's Alaskan Husky.

save money in the long run. With some generic brands, you must feed twice as much or more to get the same nutrition, and still will not get the same results as you would with a premium dog food.

There are plenty of great premium dog foods on the market, many made by companies whose names you probably recognize. You should choose a dog food that is easily available so that you don't have to drive all over town looking for your dog's food because the pet boutique where you normally buy it is closed.

You can recognize a premium dog food by its ingredients and its digestibility. The first ingredient on the list should be the protein source of the dog food, and should be an animal protein such as chicken, beef by-products or poultry meal, rather than soy, corn gluten meal or bone meal. Dogs use animal protein more efficiently than plant proteins, and overall the quality of animal protein is better. (More on this later in this chapter.)

The digestibility of a dog food is usually not stated on the package, but you can contact the manufacturer and ask them about the digestibility of their dog foods. Dog food that is over 80 percent digestible should be considered a premium dog food.

Whichever dog food you buy, be sure to purchase one that is complete and balanced. This means the dog food has all the necessary nutrients and that they are balanced so as not to cause a deficiency. Complete and balanced dog foods will have a label stating that the dog food meets or exceeds the requirements as set forth by AAFCO (the American Association of Feed Control Officials). AAFCO has established guidelines for all animal feeds. Most major dog food companies comply with AAFCO's guidelines, but you should still check the package to be sure.

Finally, choose a dog food that your dog likes. This is absolutely not trivial. The best nutrition in the world isn't worth anything if your dog won't eat it.

DRY, CANNED, SEMI-MOIST OR FROZEN?

Now that you know you need to buy premium dog food, your next step is to determine what form the dog food should take. Most premium dog foods tend to be dry or canned, but a few are available frozen. We'll look at dry food, canned food, semi-moist food, and frozen food.

- **Dry food:** Pound for pound, dry food is the most economical choice. Most dog foods come in a dried form. It's easy to handle and relatively easy to store. Dry food tends to come in the most varieties, too. On the negative side, dry food is not as palatable as other forms and some dogs may turn up their noses at it. Shelf life is not as great as canned food, because most dog foods now use natural preservatives such as tocopherols (vitamin E) to prevent rancidity.

- **Canned food:** Canned food is very palatable and many owners mix canned and dried food to make the dry food more palatable. Canned food often has more protein and fewer grain products (but not always). It has an excellent storage life. However, canned food is expensive when compared to dry, and much of what you pay for is water and processing. You must usually feed more canned food than you would dry food.

- **Semi-moist food:** This food usually comes in the shape of hamburger patties or moist nuggets. Semi-moist food is extremely palatable, but I don't recommend it as a daily diet because most semi-soft foods use sugar or corn syrup and lots of preservatives to keep them soft. They usually have some sort of artificial color added to them as well. For the amount of food you must feed, they can be quite expensive.

This is probably a dog's idea of good frozen food,
but I don't recommend Ben and Jerry's as a dog food.

- **Frozen food:** This type of dog food is relatively new. It's made
  from meat and is highly palatable, but it can be expensive. Like
  canned food, you're paying for the water, but you're also paying
  for storage. You'll need freezer space and it's highly perishable,
  because it has no preservatives. It must be kept frozen until used.

NUTRIENTS IN A DOG'S DIET

Nutrition is vitally important to all dogs, but especially puppies, pregnant and lactating females, show dogs and canine athletes. Dogs require
protein, fat, carbohydrates, vitamins, minerals and water to remain
healthy. A good diet can help prevent some diseases and health conditions. Good nutrition may help a dog live a longer and healthier life.

Think of nutrition as building blocks: These blocks can either be
made of straw or brick, depending on what you feed your dog. Good
nutrition won't make a mediocre dog a superstar, but it will make your
dog the best he can possibly be.

Your dog's food provides not only the building blocks for the dog's
body, but also the energy he needs. The dog's body converts the calories in his food into energy, which he needs to move his body and
support his metabolism. Without this energy, your dog couldn't breathe,

his heart couldn't pump blood, and his body couldn't regulate his temperature. He requires food that his body can convert into energy and can use readily.

Three major nutrients provide energy. These are protein, carbohydrates and fats. Each has a crucial role in a dog's diet.

Protein

Protein provides four calories of energy per gram and provides the building blocks for muscles, bone, organs and connective tissue. It is the main component of enzymes, hormones and antibodies. It helps with muscle repair, to build and maintain plasma volume and red blood cells, and to help working dogs store energy.

Protein is composed of 23 *amino acids*. Of these 23, a dog's body can manufacture 13. The other 10 amino acids, called essential amino acids, must come from the dog's food. A protein source with all 10 essential amino acids is said to be a complete protein source. Protein sources without all 10 are said to be incomplete protein sources.

Feed your dog a high-quality dog food for good nutrition and a beautiful coat, like Zoe's.

The amino acids must be balanced in such a way that the dog gets enough protein for his body. Because dogs are carnivores, they digest and use protein from animal products better than from plant sources. Good sources of protein include meat (chicken and poultry included), eggs, meat meal, meat by-products and meat by-product meals.

According to AAFCO guidelines, puppy food must have a minimum of 22 percent protein and adult food must have 18 percent protein on a dry-matter basis. (Dry matter means the nutritional values are measured according to the mass of the dog food, minus the weight of any added water. It's a way to compare canned food to dry food.)

Fat

Fat is an energy-dense nutrient at nine calories of energy per gram. High-quality fat sources include animal fat—unlike us, dogs generally do not build up plaque in their arteries and do not need to worry about their cholesterol intake. Fat maintains a healthy skin and coat, helps protect and insulate vital organs, and is required to transport fat-soluble vitamins such as A, D, E and K.

Dog food usually uses a mixture of saturated (solid) and unsaturated (liquid) fats. Unsaturated fat tends to turn rancid more quickly. According to AAFCO guidelines, puppy food must have a minimum of 8 percent fat and adult food must have 5 percent fat on a dry-matter basis.

Carbohydrates

Carbohydrates provide four calories of energy per gram. Because dogs are primarily carnivores, they need far fewer carbohydrates than humans. In fact, AAFCO doesn't have a minimum requirement for carbohydrates, which means a dog can live without them.

WHAT ABOUT TABLE SCRAPS?

Are table scraps good for your dog? In a word, no! Table scraps are often the inedible portions of your meal and are loaded with fat, salt and carbohydrates, but have very little nutritive value. At one time, people used to feed their dogs nothing but table scraps, but then, we don't know how long the dogs lived in those days. Since people's lifespans were much shorter than they are today, we can assume that dogs didn't live that long, either.

However, carbohydrates do provide energy and fiber and facilitate replacement of fuels within the body's cells. Fiber also helps in water absorption and in maintaining good bowel movements.

Water

When we think of nutrients, we seldom think of water. But without water, a dog wouldn't live very long. A dog can go without food for a long time, but will die quickly without water.

Every major system within a dog's body uses water. Your dog loses water through respiration, urination, defecation and through the sweat glands on his paws. If he loses too much, he will become dehydrated. Always have fresh water available at all times and make sure it comes from a known and clean source. Water from creeks and streams may contain microorganisms such as *Giardia* that can cause severe diarrhea and vomiting.

HOW TO READ DOG FOOD LABELS

Dog food labels can be confusing. When you pick up a package of dog food, you'll see information that is required by the Food and Drug Administration (FDA). It includes:

- Product name
- Manufacturer's name and address
- Net weight
- Guaranteed analysis
- Nutritional adequacy statement
- Feeding directions

The guaranteed analysis contains:

- Minimum percentage of crude protein
- Minimum percentage of crude fat
- Maximum percentage of crude fiber
- Maximum percentage of moisture or water

These percentages are listed "as is" or "as fed," sometimes called "by-weight." ("By-weight" means the nutritional percentages are calculated as a percentage of the total mass of the food, which includes water, ash and fillers—none of which have any caloric value.) Some dog foods

> ## HOW MUCH FOOD?
>
> Start with the dog food manufacturer's feeding instructions for your
> dog's weight and age, and split the daily ration into two or three meals
> a day. Usually the amounts recommended on the package are more than
> what an average dog needs, but it's a good start. If your dog doesn't fin-
> ish each meal in about 20 minutes, or if he is gaining weight (rather
> than maintaining a healthy weight), cut back the portions until your
> dog is maintaining a healthy weight.

will list ash as well. These percentages guarantee a certain amount of
protein and fat. However, they don't guarantee the quality of the ingredients. Protein can be from indigestible or digestible ingredients.

There is other information that the dog food manufacturer may put
on the label, including calories per serving and digestibility, but this is
voluntary and is at the sole discretion of the company.

When you look at the ingredient list on a dog food, the ingredients
are listed according to weight. In other words, the first ingredient is the
most common ingredient; it is followed by the second most common,
and so on. Look for a food that has a meat protein source first, followed
by other ingredients.

So, if the first ingredient is chicken, does that mean the food is
mostly chicken? Not necessarily. Suppose the first five ingredients in a
dog food are chicken, corn gluten meal, wheat middlings, corn, poultry
fat (preserved with BHA). The corn gluten meal, wheat middlings and
corn, combined, may outweigh the chicken. Also, "chicken" includes
the water that is in the chicken, while chicken meal and chicken by-
product meal have the water and fat extracted—leaving more protein
per gram. Technically, chicken meal could have a higher percentage of
available protein than chicken, pound for pound.

HOMEMADE DIETS: FACTS AND FALLACIES

Homemade and raw food diets are becoming extremely popular with
a small but vocal group of dog owners. Most popular are the raw diets,
including the BARF (Bones and Raw Food) diet. Proponents of these
diets claim they cure everything from allergies to cancer. These folks
back up their statements with anecdotal data.

The problem with homemade diets is that many of them are not scientifically developed or tested to be nutritionally balanced. What may look good on paper often falls short in real life. Dog food companies spend millions of dollars on research to improve their dog food every year. That bag of premium dog food is the culmination of decades of research and testing—how close do you think you can get to optimal nutrition by giving your dog a chicken wing and some cut-up vegetables? Indeed, studies published in the *Journal of the American Veterinary Medical Association* have shown that homemade diets are often inconsistent and may cause dangerous imbalances in vitamins and minerals, as well as test positive for harmful bacteria.

There *are* valid reasons for creating a homemade diet. One is that your dog is allergic to or intolerant of certain ingredients in dog food and you can't find a suitable commercial diet; another is that your dog needs a special diet due to a serious medical condition. Yet another valid reason is that you may need to formulate your own dog food because where you live, you do not have access to premium dog food formulated in accordance with AAFCO guidelines. The fourth valid reason for formulating your own food is that you have high-performance working dogs, such as sled dogs, and their nutritional requirements exceed even high-performance dog food. In all of these situations, you should be working with a veterinary nutritionist to formulate an optimum diet for your dog.

So, what are the facts and fallacies regarding homemade diets? Let's look at some statements from the proponents of homemade diets.

- **Home-cooked or raw diets can cure diseases.** There is no scientific evidence that home-cooked or raw diets cure anything. Dogs who have allergies or intolerances to certain ingredients in dog food may do well on a homemade diet because the owner has left out the offending ingredients. You would see the same or better results if the dog was on a hypoallergenic diet that did not have the offending ingredients. In fact, some homemade diets may *cause* health problems due to the presence of *E. coli* and *Salmonella* bacteria.

- **Dogs live longer on raw diets.** Again, there is no evidence that a dog lives longer on a raw food diet—or even a homemade cooked diet. I have two dogs who are still alive at 16 years old who are fed commercial diets. (The average life span of dogs of this type is around 13 to 15 years.)

- **Raw bones won't hurt a dog.** Ask any veterinarian and they will tell you horror stories about removing bones from the intestines and mouths of dogs. While wolves eat bones in the wild, they normally eat the bones along with the skin and hair, which helps protect their mouth and internal organs against rough edges. And if a wolf had a perforated intestine or a blockage, he would simply die.

- **Raw food diets mimic what a wolf eats, and are therefore more natural.** Not really. Wolves don't eat celery, carrots and potatoes. They eat organs, intestines, contents of the prey animal's stomach, muscle meat, skin and hair. A chicken wing or a cow femur with some meat on it, mixed with fruits and vegetables, doesn't mimic what a wolf eats at all. And while a dog's digestive system is similar to a wolf's, a wolf generally doesn't live very long in the wild—so why would you want to mimic his diet?

- **I know what to feed my kids—why not my dog?** Do you feed your kids cereal (fortified with vitamins) in the morning? Do you give your kids vitamins? Do you feed prepackaged foods that are nutritionally enhanced? If you do, someone has already done the research for you.

- **Raw diets have better-quality ingredients.** This may be true, depending on the dog food, but in many cases raw food is not complete and balanced. So any quality advantage is far outweighed by nutritional deficiencies.

   If you decide to feed your dog a homemade diet, be sure to have it analyzed by a veterinary nutritionist to ensure that the diet is complete and balanced.

TREATS

So far, I've covered what type of dog food to feed your dog, but nothing about the fun stuff. What about treats? Treats are good if you limit them to no more than 10 percent of your dog's total calories for the day. Treats can include people food (within moderation), dog biscuits and other dog treats. Many dog treats are loaded with fat and calories, so use them sparingly. I prefer giving my dogs hard, crunchy biscuits as a treat, because they help keep my dogs' teeth healthy.

UNSAFE FOODS

Surprisingly, foods that are safe for you can be poisonous to your dog. Here is a partial list of dangerous foods:

- **Chocolate:** contains theobromine, a substance poisonous to dogs; dark chocolate is more poisonous than milk chocolate, but any chocolate is bad for a dog.
- **Alcohol:** very toxic to dogs, due to their body mass; very little alcohol can cause alcohol poisoning in dogs.
- **Onions:** can cause a type of anemia.
- **Raisins and grapes:** have been known to cause renal failure and death.
- **Raw salmon from the Northwest:** carries a fluke that can kill dogs.
- **Raw pork:** may carry a dangerous parasite called trichinosis.
- **Raw egg whites:** contain a substance that will cause a biotin deficiency.

PUDGY POOCHES

Obesity is a growing problem in dogs. Most pets are overweight and many are obese. Obesity leads to many health problems, including diabetes, arthritis and congestive heart failure. Obesity often shortens a dog's life span.

How do you know if your dog is on the heavy side? Have your dog stand beside you. Put your thumbs on his spine and feel down along his ribs. If you have an amazing ribless dog or can barely feel his ribs through the padding, your dog is obese.

Always seek your vet's help before putting your dog on a weight loss diet or exercise program. Your vet can prescribe a prescription diet. Several dog food manufacturers, including Purina, Hill's and Waltham, offer diet foods available through your vet.

Another potential weight loss food is the "lite" version of dog foods. A new regulation implemented by AAFCO requires that all dog food labeled "lite" or "low calorie" must contain no more than 3,100 calories per kilo (a kilo is about 2.2 pounds). That's still pretty hefty, so consult with your vet to see if there is anything else you can do to trim your pudgy pooch.

Please note that these diet dog foods work fine only if you feed your dog the same amount you would with normal food. It does no good to feed "lite" foods if you overfeed.

Exercise will help trim your dog to his proper weight, but start slowly. It doesn't have to be a lot—start with a short walk or a game of fetch every day, and gradually build up.

• •

CHAPTER 16

GROOMING YOUR MUTT

Your dog will have healthier skin and hair, look beautiful and smell sweet if you keep her well-groomed. A clean dog is enjoyable to touch and have around. A dirty dog is, well, a dirty dog.

Grooming isn't just brushing and combing or bathing. Cleaning ears, clipping nails and brushing your dog's teeth are all part of grooming. In this chapter, we'll cover grooming from nose to tail, and everything in-between.

YOUR MUTT'S WASH-AND-WEAR COAT

With a mixed breed's coat, you may get the proverbial mixed bag. Depending on the mix, your dog may have a single coat (without an undercoat) or a double coat. Her hair may be terrierlike or Poodlelike (which requires trimming), or may be Huskylike with a thick undercoat. Is it short and sleek like a Labrador Retriever, or long and fluffy like a Samoyed? Maybe it's all of the above!

How often you groom your dog depends on the type of coat, whether she is shedding seasonally (all dogs shed some all year round) and whether she is dirty. Naturally, a dirty dog requires grooming. Dog with single coats may need extra clipping and dogs with double coats may need extra grooming, especially when they shed heavily. Regardless of the coat, you'll need to brush and comb your dog at least once a week. Dogs with long hair that tangles easily will require more frequent brushing. Dogs with short coats can probably get by with a quick brushing. Dogs with double coats shed heavily once or twice a year, depending on what breeds they're mixed with and your climate, and will need daily brushing during those seasonal sheds.

Grooming Tools

You'll need some standard grooming supplies for your dog. These include the basic brushes and combs, and also things that might seem extravagant, such as a canine blow dryer and a grooming table. These items are optional, but will certainly make your job much easier. A grooming table will help save your back and dog blow dryers won't burn your dog's skin (blow dryers made for humans are just too hot for dogs).

- Slicker brush
- Zoom Groom or curry brush (for dogs with a short coat)
- Undercoat rake (for dogs with a double coat)
- Flea comb
- Long-tooth comb
- Mat splitter or mat rake (for dogs with a double coat)
- Electric clipper (for dogs with a single coat)
- Shears (for dogs with a single coat)
- Thinning shears (for dogs with a single coat)
- Grooming table with noose (*never* leave your dog on it)
- Blow dryer for dogs
- Shampoo formulated for dogs
- Cream rinse formulated for dogs
- Nail clippers or nail grinder
- Styptic powder
- Toothpaste and toothbrush for dogs

Brushing and Combing

How you brush your dog depends on her coat, but you should always start by brushing the hair until it is smooth and untangling any mats (use a mat splitter or a detangler solution, don't just pull at them). Never use scissors to cut out a mat! You can severely cut your dog's skin even if you are careful. If your dog has too many mats, bring her to a groomer, who may have to use clippers to cut away the matted fur.

Next, brush your dog's hair against the grain. This helps stimulate oils in the coat. Then brush the dog's hair back into place.

STABLER

A grooming table makes it much easier to groom your dog.

Baths

Although it's tempting, you should never bathe a dog without first brushing her out. Some coat types are prone to tangles and matts, which certainly become worse if you bathe the dog. Instead, brush your dog out and then bathe her with a good pH-balanced shampoo for dogs. Do not use shampoo for humans; it can dry out a dog's skin. Follow it with a cream rinse made for dogs, and rinse thoroughly—then rinse again.

You may want to consider putting a small piece of cotton in each ear, so that the water doesn't get in them. Be sure the water is tepid to the touch. And rinse your dog really well, because the soap and cream rinse will attract dirt.

Some dogs hate baths. There are restraining nooses that can be attached with suction cups to the bathroom wall so you can keep your dog in the tub while you wash her. (*Never* leave a dog unattended in one!)

Pat your dog down with thick towels and keep her away from drafts. Use a dog blow dryer to dry her, and brush her one more time.

Clipping

Unless you're a pro at clipping, you might want to leave that chore to a professional (see below), who can shape your dog's coat into a nice style. The groomer can also show you how to maintain the cut between grooming sessions.

Short-coated dogs like Sadie are wash-and-wear.

If you want to learn how to clip your dog's fur, ask an expert. Some trainers and groomers will be happy to help you. Other people to ask include breeders and show people with breeds that have single coats. Even though your dog isn't purebred, they can show you a nice pet cut that would work with your dog's coat.

SHOULD YOU USE A PROFESSIONAL GROOMER?

If you don't have the time or if your dog has a high-maintenance coat, grooming can be a daunting task. If you're a busy person, paying a groomer to bathe and clip your dog once every two weeks or once a month isn't extravagant—it's a necessity! Be honest with yourself; if you just don't have time to groom your dog, have an expert do it.

But don't wait until your dog is filthy and her fur is matted. The groomer will charge you more for that. Also, if your dog has a long coat or requires more clipping, it will cost more than if she has a shorter coat or her coat has been maintained.

How do you find a good professional groomer? Ask other dog owners which groomers they use and if they would recommend them. Ask your vet who they would recommend. Some vets even have a groomer on staff.

Once you find a groomer you're interested in, contact them and ask what certifications they have. Although there are many good groomers without any certification, a certified groomer has met certain minimum standards. Ask what services they perform (some groomers will trim nails, clean ears and express anal sacs). Ask the groomer how many clients they have regularly.

Be aware that some groomers tranquilize dogs, especially if the dog is aggressive or difficult to work on. If your dog is prone to seizures, certain tranquilizers can cause seizures. In most cases, it's better to use a groomer who doesn't tranquilize.

Once you've prescreened a groomer, visit the grooming shop. If the groomer is especially busy, you'll see hair and water on the floor, but otherwise the grooming shop should be neat and orderly. Watch how the groomer and staff (if there are any) handle the dogs. Are they gentle or rough? If there are cage dryers, does the groomer check on the dogs in them frequently? Some heated cage dryers have overheated dogs. Finally, does the groomer have enough room to put all the dogs in crates that are big enough?

*Even mutts deserve a great hairdo. A professional
groomer can give you professional results.*

Choose a groomer carefully, and not just on price. Your dog will spend some intense time at the groomer's, and you want the experience to be as pleasant as possible.

DOGGIE DENTAL CARE

Dogs have dental problems such as tartar and gum disease like humans. Infected teeth can cause severe health problems, including heart problems. Cavities in a dog's mouth are rare, because dogs don't eat much sugar; give a dog ice cream every day and she will get cavities, too.

Many vets recommend brushing your dog's teeth every day with toothpaste specially formulated for dogs (toothpaste for humans is entirely unsuitable for dogs). Many dog owners don't have the time or patience to do that, but I do recommend brushing your dog's teeth twice a week to reduce plaque, which leads to tartar. If your dog has good teeth (and healthy teeth and gums largely depend on genetics and diet), you might be able to get away with brushing her teeth less, but that's inadvisable.

Think brushing a dog's teeth is silly? Professional teeth cleaning requires anesthesia and its associated risks—not to mention expense!

Brushing Your Mutt's Teeth

If your dog isn't used to having her mouth handled, you won't be able to brush her teeth. Start by holding your dog's head gently, flipping up her lip and briefly touching her teeth and gums. Do this gently and praise her. Practice this often, so she becomes used to you touching her mouth.

After she is used to this kind of handling, get a soft washcloth and wet a corner of it. Now, using your finger, gently massage your dog's gums with the tip of the washcloth. You need not go any further than this, but for the full dental treatment, buy a toothbrush and toothpaste for dogs. These are available at pet supply stores and through mail order and Internet pet supply companies. You must use toothpaste formulated for pets, because human toothpaste is poisonous to dogs. Most pet toothpastes are chicken or malt flavored, which makes the process a little easier.

Recognizing a Tooth or Gum Problem

Hopefully, your dog will go through life without a tooth or gum problem. If you feed her good food and give her plenty of chewing toys, you should minimize the need for teeth cleaning. However, just as some people have bad teeth no matter what they do, so do some dogs. Learn to recognize the warning signs on dental disease. Take your dog to the vet if you see any of the following:

- Loss of appetite
- Sudden, unexpected chewing on inappropriate items
- Bad breath
- Nasal discharge
- Red, swollen gums
- A lump above or below a particular tooth

CLEANING YOUR DOG'S EARS

Some dogs develop ear problems frequently, others never seem to have a problem. Dogs with ears that hang down seem to have a predilection for ear infections and injuries. Those drop ears make an ideal place for bacteria to grow and mites to hide.

Regardless of whether they're prick ears or drop ears or something in-between, your dog's ears should be clean and sweet smelling. If there is an odor, your dog may have an infection.

Clean your dog's ears once a week. Use a mild ear cleaning solution made for dogs. Squeeze some into your dog's ears and then gently massage the outside of the ear canal. Take sterile gauze or sponges and gently wipe out the excess (do not poke anything into the ear canal). Don't leave any behind or it could lead to an ear infection.

Don't use insecticides or mite treatments on the ears, as this can cause irritation. If you suspect ear mites, see your vet for the appropriate treatment.

Recognizing an Ear Problem

If you see any of these signs of potential ear problems, it's time to visit the vet:

- Blisters or abrasions on the ears
- The dog yelps when you touch her ears
- Ears are crusty or red
- Excessive waxy buildup
- Foul odor from the ears
- Red or black waxy buildup
- Your dog scratches or paws at her ears, or shakes her head

CLIPPING YOUR DOG'S NAILS

Most dogs hate having their nails clipped. You can minimize the stress by getting your dog used to you handling her feet. Start by gently touching and picking up each foot for a few seconds. Gradually increase the time you hold your dog's feet.

Clip your dog's nails once a week to keep them short and healthy. Long nails may break and cause pain, and can splay the dog's foot.

When you start clipping your dog's nails, use a dog nail clipper and snip off just a small portion of the nail at a time. If the nail feels spongy or hard to cut, stop immediately. You can use a nail grinder, which will help file the nail instead. (Some dogs handle the nail grinder better than the clippers, too.) Dogs have a pink part inside the nail, which is where the nerves and blood supply are. This is called the *quick*. If you cut into the quick, your dog will let you know in no uncertain terms—and won't want you near her paws again! It hurts, and she'll also bleed profusely. Because many dogs' nails are dark, you have to make an educated guess about where the quick is.

Have styptic powder or sodium nitrate on hand, in case you do cut the quick. Packing the nail with styptic powder will stop the bleeding. You can buy styptic powder at pet supply stores or through pet supply catalogs. In a pinch, you can also use cornstarch.

ANAL SACS

Dog have two glands at the four o'clock and eight o'clock positions around their anus. These usually empty when the dog defecates, but occasionally they become overfull or impacted.

If your dog starts scooting around on her rear or chewing the fur on her rear or tail, she may have full or impacted anal sacs. This can be very painful, and can lead to serious infections. They need to be emptied

The best times to empty the anal sacs are when you are bathing the dog. The secretions are smellier than a skunk and you'll want to clean her off after you express them.

Fold up a wad of paper towels and place them over your dog's anus. Now press gently on the four and eight o'clock positions. The glands should express themselves. If the problem persists, bring your dog to the vet. She could have impacted anal glands, which your vet may have to express.

CHAPTER 17

CHOOSING A VETERINARIAN

Choosing a veterinarian is very important for your dog's health. Finding the right vet for both you and your dog may take a little searching, but it is well worth it. Your veterinarian is your partner in ensuring the health of your dog.

There are plenty of competent vets, but not every one has the same philosophy or bedside manner. Some veterinarians stick to conventional medicine; others use holistic techniques. Some specialize in purebred dogs or in cats or reptiles; others enjoy working with all pets. Some have expertise in specific areas, such as oncology or neurology; others are general practitioners.

NOT ALL VETERINARIANS ARE ALIKE

What kind of veterinarian should you look for? It depends on what kind of services you need. If you drive around your neighborhood, chances are you'll find a veterinarian in a local strip mall next to the grocery store, the drug store and the local fast-food takeout. Some veterinarians have offices in pet supply stores, as well. But are they any good?

It depends on what you're looking for. Nowadays, vets offer a variety of services, from emergency clinics to specialists to boarding and grooming. Some vets offer mobile clinics and make house calls, while others offer fast, convenient service and low prices. But price should not be the only consideration when you're looking for a vet.

When you start your search, you'll find a wide variety of veterinary establishments, including:

- **Veterinary clinics:** Vet clinics may have as few as one or as many as five or more vets. These clinics have set office hours and may or may not handle emergencies.

- **Animal hospitals:** These hospitals usually employ a large number of vets and may have specialists. They may have their own testing facilities that a smaller clinic can't afford. They may handle complex surgeries and emergencies that can't be treated anywhere else.
- **Emergency clinics:** These clinics are for emergencies only. They usually handle after-hours calls and tend to be expensive.
- **Low-cost clinics:** This is a relatively new type of vet clinic. The purpose of most low-cost clinics is to provide routine services (vaccinations, heartworm tests, spay/neuters) at a low cost so that everyone can afford them. These clinics make up for the lower price in higher volume. These clinics generally don't have the facilities to handle emergencies or complex diagnoses.
- **Mobile clinics:** These mobile clinics usually have very limited facilities and are affiliated with an animal hospital or a veterinary clinic. They offer convenience to the pet owner.

FINDING THE BEST VET FOR YOUR MUTT

Finding the right veterinarian isn't difficult, but you may have to do a bit of looking. A good referral is worth a lot. Talk first with your dog-owning friends. Most will recommend a local veterinarian they like. Sometimes the shelter where you adopted your dog can recommend a veterinarian nearby. Other people to ask include dog trainers or groomers. Other places to look for veterinarians include the Yellow Pages in the phone book, your state's veterinary association, or the American Veterinary Medical Association (AVMA), which will have a list of veterinarians near you (you'll find contact information in Appendix A).

Think about what's important to you. Many clinics offer services besides veterinary services such as grooming and boarding for their clients. This may be important to you if you have a puppy who requires intensive grooming or if you need to board your puppy at any time. When you know what you want, call the veterinarians you are considering and find out what services they offer. The following questions will also help you decide which of the veterinarians may be right for you:

- What hours is the clinic open?
- How many veterinarians are in the practice?
- Does the clinic handle emergencies? Is there an after-hours number where you can reach the veterinarian or an on-call veterinarian?

- Does the clinic offer boarding?
- Do the veterinarians make house calls?
- Is there a groomer available?
- Do the veterinarians have their own lab equipment or do they need to send out for tests?
- Are the veterinarians specialists? What are they specialists in?
- Is this a clinic or a hospital?
- Do the veterinarians offer a multi-pet discount on certain services?
- Have the veterinarians worked with mixed breeds quite a bit?
- Does the clinic offer payment plans if your dog has an expensive emergency?

Once you narrow the list of possible veterinarians, it's time to visit the clinic. Don't drop by unannounced, because some days are busier than others. Call and ask when it would be convenient to visit.

When you visit, look around. Is the staff pleasant and friendly? Is the clinic clean and orderly? If there has been an emergency or if this is a particularly busy day, the clinic might be messy, but the overall appearance should leave a good impression.

HOLISTIC VETERINARIANS

Holistic medicine is becoming very popular in our mainstream culture. If you've ever taken herbal supplements, visited a chiropractor or acupuncturist or received a therapeutic massage, you've experienced holistic medicine (also called *alternative* or *natural medicine*). It is also rapidly gaining ground in the veterinary community.

Does holistic medicine work? *Maybe*. Without hard scientific research, some forms of holistic medicine may be more reliable than others. Nobody knows for sure. My own experience, which is only anecdotal, is that *some* holistic medicine works. Most holistic medicine can work in conjunction with more conventional treatments, so it isn't necessarily an "either/or" situation. Most vets are open-minded enough not to object if you use holistic treatments in conjunction with conventional treatments.

Unlike the situation in human medicine, most veterinary holistic practitioners are also veterinarians. That means they have had both conventional and holistic training, and are in the perfect position to combine both kinds of therapy to come up with a treatment that works best for your dog.

If you decide a holistic vet is right for you and your dog, you have a bit more work to do. Choosing a holistic vet is a lot like choosing a regular vet, except not all holistic vets are skilled in all modalities. You must first decide what modalities you want to use on your pet. For example, if you want a vet who knows acupuncture as well as conventional medicine, you need to contact the International Veterinary Acupuncture Society (you'll find contact information for a number of holistic veterinary groups in Appendix A) for a list of approved veterinary acupuncturists in your area, and then ask the vets if they also practice conventional veterinary medicine. Once you know what you're looking for, you can search for the right holistic practitioner.

Ask other like-minded pet owners who they take their pets to. See if their recommendations correspond with the lists you obtain from the various holistic veterinary organizations. If you go to any holistic practitioners for yourself, ask them who they take their pets to.

When selecting a vet, remember that not everyone who claims to do holistic veterinary medicine is an expert. Even holistic experts agree that there are charlatans in this field trying to make a quick buck. Choose a licensed veterinarian who is certified in and has practiced your choice of modalities for many years as your pet's primary practitioner.

YOUR MUTT'S FIRST VET VISIT

Your dog's first visit to the vet need not be traumatic. When you make an appointment, ask the receptionist if you should bring anything. Most vets would like any medical records you may have on your dog. If your dog or puppy comes from a shelter or another owner, you should at least have a vaccination record. Some vets would like you to bring in a stool sample. Be sure to bring it in a labeled plastic bag. (No one wants a nasty surprise!)

If this is a routine office visit or your puppy's first visit, the veterinarian should give your dog a thorough exam. He should listen to your dog's heart and check him over for any problems. Most vets will ask what you are feeding your dog and make recommendations. Your vet will most likely discuss proper dog or puppy health care and the benefits of spaying or neutering.

Now is the time to ask any questions about your dog's health. Don't feel silly asking questions—most vets have heard them all before, and are happy to answer. If you don't understand something your vet says, ask!

Your vet will also discuss vaccinations with you. Depending on your vet's philosophy concerning vaccinations, you may be vaccinating your dog or puppy at this time. Follow your vet's advice concerning vaccinations. (You'll find more information on vaccinations in Chapter 18.)

PET HEALTH INSURANCE

One trip to the vet and you may be wondering why pet health care costs so much. A simple checkup and vaccinations may cost $100 or more. Have a series of tests run or surgery, and you're likely to see a bill in the hundreds of dollars. Some kinds of treatment can cost thousands of dollars. Veterinary care is actually a bargain if you compare the cost to similar services for humans. This is not much of a consolation if you're stuck with a bill you can't pay.

Pet health insurance works a lot like human health insurance. Depending on the type of insurance, most pet health insurance covers major catastrophes such as accidents and illnesses. Some, such as VPI PetCare and Petshealth, cover accidents and illnesses, including office calls, lab fees, X-rays, surgery and general treatments. Most of these treatments have a cap, so the payout for cancer, for example, may be limited to $3,000.

Some health insurance plans cover vaccinations and routine medical care either at a discount or for an extra fee. VPI, for example, offers vaccination and routine care coverage for a set price above the standard premium. Petshealth offers two wellness programs that include various levels of preventive care.

Many pet health insurance companies don't cover preexisting conditions or hereditary or congenital defects such as hip dysplasia, entropion or other potentially expensive problems.

If you decide you want to purchase a plan, be sure to choose one that is underwritten by an insurance company that is rated A or higher. You don't what to pay for a policy, only to have the company go under before you can get a claim paid. Longevity is also important—look for a company that has been in business along time. In Appendix A you'll find a list of pet health insurance companies. This is not an endorsement of any particular company, and is intended only as information.

• •

CHAPTER 18

PREVENTIVE CARE

When you think of your dog's health, you may be inclined to think first of your dog's veterinarian. But in reality, your veterinarian probably will not be the first person to notice something is wrong with your mutt. Your vet can make recommendations and examine your dog, but you are ultimately responsible for your dog's health and well-being.

Keeping your dog healthy begins with preventive care. Keeping up on her vaccinations and heartworm medications is one way to prevent serious illnesses. Spaying or neutering your dog will help reduce the likelihood of several types of cancers. Learning how to examine your dog, how to take her temperature and how to give medications are all very important for the health of your dog.

VACCINATIONS AND IMMUNITY

During their first few weeks of life, puppies get a natural immunity against diseases from the antibodies in their mother's colostrum—the first milk. However, this immunity is only temporary. The maternal antibodies begin to fade some time between the puppy's fifth and 16th week.

Veterinarians try to vaccinate the puppy after the maternal antibodies fade but before the puppy can become exposed to any deadly diseases. The problem is that it's hard to know when the maternal antibodies fade, because it varies with each puppy. If a vaccination is given too soon, the material antibodies will interfere and the vaccine will not produce immunity. If the vaccination is given too late, the puppy has a long period when she is at risk. This is why it is very important to follow your veterinarian's recommendations regarding vaccinations.

If your dog is an adult, vaccinations are still important. Certain diseases, such as rabies and distemper, can affect any dog at any age. Your veterinarian can recommend an appropriate vaccine schedule for your dog.

Vaccination Choices

In this section I will list the vaccines that are currently available. Unless your dog is at high risk for certain diseases, she probably does not need all these vaccinations. What vaccinations your dog needs should be decided by you and your veterinarian, based on your dog's age and health, and the area of the country you live in.

Many veterinarians vaccinate once a year, but the current trend in veterinary medicine is to vaccinate every three years. In some cases, over-vaccinating has led to autoimmune disorders in dogs and cats. Talk to your veterinarian about a vaccination regimen that is right for your individual dog.

Rabies

Rabies has been feared throughout the ages, and with good reason! Rabies is caused by a virus and is nearly always fatal. It is contagious to humans and is transmitted through the dog's saliva—either through a bite or through wounds. The incubation period varies anywhere from three weeks to three months or more.

Rabies takes two forms—dumb (paralytic) and furious—and both affect the central nervous system. In dumb rabies, the dog's throat becomes paralyzed, causing drooling and the inability to swallow. Furious rabies is the classic "mad dog" form, where the dog becomes vicious and attacks without provocation. Furious rabies eventually progresses to the paralytic stage and death follows within a few days.

Most municipalities require dogs to have rabies vaccinations. Most vaccines are the three-year variety, meaning that the pharmaceutical company that makes it has tested it and certifies that it is effective in dogs for up to three years.

Canine Distemper

Distemper is highly contagious among dogs and may be transmitted through the air, on shoes or on clothing. It is nearly always fatal. Distemper starts with a yellow-gray discharge from the nose and eyes, high fever, dry cough and lethargy. It may progress to appetite loss, diarrhea and vomiting. Distemper may affect the intestinal tract or may attack the nervous system, causing seizures and convulsions. Some dogs may have the hardening of the pads, hence the name "hardpad disease."

Canine Adenovirus 2

Canine adenovirus 2 is a form of highly contagious kennel cough. Dogs who contract kennel cough have a harsh, dry cough and may sound like they are gagging. Unless the dog is very old or very young, kennel cough is more of a nuisance than a danger.

Infectious Canine Hepatitis

Infectious canine hepatitis is a form of adenovirus that causes fever, lethargy, jaundice, excessive thirst, vomiting, eye and nasal discharge, bloody diarrhea, hunched back, hemorrhage and conjunctivitis. Infectious canine hepatitis may attack the kidneys, liver, eyes and the lining of blood vessels. This disease may occur simultaneously with canine distemper. It's contagious to other dogs through an infected dog's urine, feces or saliva.

Canine Parainfluenza

Canine parainfluenza is another form of kennel cough. Dogs who contract kennel cough have a harsh, dry cough and may sound like they are gagging. Unless the dog is very old or young, kennel cough is more of a nuisance than a danger.

Leptospirosis

Leptospirosis is a bacterial infection that causes high fever, frequent urination, a brown substance on the tongue, lack of appetite, kidney failure, hunched back, bloody vomit and diarrhea, mild conjunctivitis and depression. Dogs may contract leptospirosis from rats, infected water supplies and other infected dogs. It is contagious to humans. It can be fatal to dogs, and more deadly forms have also caused death in people.

Canine Parvovirus

Canine parvovirus is a dangerous virus that causes severe, bloody diarrhea, vomiting, dehydration, high fever and depression. Half of all puppies who contract it die. Canine parvovirus is highly infectious in dogs and is transmitted through fecal matter. The virus can live up to one year in the soil and can be carried on shoes or paws.

Canine Coronavirus

Coronavirus looks a lot like a milder form of parvovirus, and is transmitted through fecal material. Both parvovirus and coronavirus may infect a dog simultaneously.

Bordetella bronchiseptica

Bordetella bronchiseptica is a form of kennel cough. Dogs who contract kennel cough have a harsh, dry cough and may sound like they are gagging. Unless the dog is very old or very young, bordetella is more of a nuisance than a danger.

Lyme Disease (Borellosis)

Lyme disease causes fever, lameness, loss of appetite and fatigue in both animals and people who are bitten by infected deer ticks. Lyme disease is fairly common along the East Coast and Upper Midwest in the United States, and continues to spread.

Giardiasis

Giardiasis is caused by *Giardia,* a microscopic organism that lives in streams. Carried by beavers and other wildlife, as well as domesticated animals, *Giardia* was once confined to the Rocky Mountains, but may now be found in any untreated water. *Giardiasis* causes severe diarrhea, vomiting and weight loss.

SPAYING AND NEUTERING

Each year millions of unwanted pets are put to death at shelters across the United States. While there are no precise figures, as a mutt owner you know firsthand how important it is to control pet overpopulation. Go into a local shelter and you'll see plenty of unwanted dogs. Mutts, sadly, make up 75 percent of them.

Many of these unwanted pets came from unplanned litters or from people who thought it might be fun or profitable to breed these dogs. Or they just didn't bother to spay or neuter their dogs, and the female "unexpectedly" became pregnant. Unfortunately, these dogs quickly became unwanted and the owner dumped the litter off at the animal shelter.

Why are there so many irresponsible dog owners? Most people are well-meaning but still believe some very outdated notions. Some people think it's better to let a bitch have one litter of puppies to "settle her temperament." Others think their male dogs will miss sex if they're neutered, or will no longer be good watchdogs. Someone once told me that keeping an intact dog is healthier.

Nothing could be farther from the truth! Dogs who are spayed or neutered are actually healthier and happier than intact dogs. Spaying and neutering reduces or eliminates the likelihood of certain types of cancer in dogs (mammary tumors, testicular cancer, ovarian cancer and anal tumors). You'll eliminate the three-week or longer estrus cycle in females and curb your male dog's urge to roam. Your dog will be more focused on you rather than on sexual urges. Dogs (both male and female) who are dominant aggressive may be easier to get along with once they are neutered or spayed. Male dogs don't lose their protective instinct when they're neutered, females aren't better behaved after they've had a litter (although they tend to be better behaved after they have been spayed) and neither sex will become fat if you watch their food intake.

Finally, some pet owners want a dog just like the dog they have. But that is impossible. Genetics is a funny thing, and in mutts, it's even stranger. But the bottom line is that your dog got half her genes from her mother and half from her father, so your best chance to get a puppy who is genetically very close to your dog is to breed her mother and her father again. And even then, the pups will end up with different combinations of genes (think about it: all the puppies in a litter have the same parents but they are not exactly alike).

Even if you end up with a puppy who looked just the same, she never would be exactly the same as your dog. That's because the personality of a dog is formed by a complex interaction between her genetics and her life experiences.

To show you how unique life is, consider the Missyplicity Project. An anonymous benefactor wanted to clone his Husky mix named Missy, and donated funds to Texas A&M University to produce an identical dog. The researchers were able to clone a cat, but discovered, after spending $3.7 million, that the calico cat they reproduced genetically was very different from the original cat, having different coloration and a different personality. This demonstrates that even with identical genetic material, the animal may not be the same. If a clone may not have the same personality or looks, how are you going to reproduce your pet by breeding two mutts?

Almost every veterinarian is proficient at neutering and spaying. The procedure can be done when the puppy is very young (eight weeks). Indeed, many shelters now have all the dogs spayed or neutered before their new owners can take them home, regardless of the puppy's age. Many shelters require that their adopted dogs are spayed or neutered. If you have concerns or worries about spaying or neutering your pet, talk to your veterinarian. They should be happy to address all your concerns.

LOW-COST SPAY/NEUTER PROGRAMS

There are many national and local programs that provide free or low-cost spay/neuter services. Generally, the national programs work with local vets to offer these services. When you contact them, they will put you in touch with a local low-cost program. Some programs include:

Friends of Animals
(800) 321-PETS
www.friendsofanimals.org

When you contact Friends of Animals, they'll send you a list of participating veterinarians in your area. You send them a check (currently $75 for a female dog, $54 for a male dog), and they send you back a certificate that you can take to any vet on their list. There are no additional costs at the vet's office.

SPAY USA
(800) 248-SPAY
www.spayusa.org

SPAY USA has more than 950 sterilization programs and clinics nationwide, with approximately 8,000 veterinarians in their network. Rates vary by region and veterinarian.

Spaying and neutering prevents unwanted litters. Mixed breeds, with the exception of dogs used for working and racing (Alaskan Huskies, for example), should never be bred. By spaying and neutering your pet, you've perhaps made a little more room in someone's home for a shelter dog who might not otherwise have been adopted.

THE HOME HEALTH EXAM

You should make it a weekly ritual to examine your dog, preferably while grooming her. Start with your dog's head and work your way back. Look for abnormalities such as bumps and lumps. If you feel a lump, check the other side of her body to see if it is normal. For example, if you feel something lumpy on the right elbow, check the left one in the same place. If there is a similar lump on the left elbow, you can safely assume those lumps are normal.

Also check:

- **Eyes:** Your dog's eyes should be clear and bright without excessive or puslike discharge, and no redness or tearing.

- **Nose:** Your dog's nose should be cool to the touch and moist (a hot and dry nose may indicate a fever). There should be no discharge or blood.

- **Ears:** Your dog's ears should be clean and sweet-smelling. Any foul odor or excessive buildup of wax indicates a possible ear problem.

- **Mouth:** Your dog's teeth should be white and clean, without tartar buildup. Your dog's breath should not be foul; if it is, it may suggest tooth or gum problems. The gums should be a healthy pink, not red and inflamed.

- **Legs:** Feel down your dog's legs to check for any lumps or bumps. Inspect the footpads for cuts and foreign objects such as foxtails. The nails should not be red or broken. If you find an unusual bump, have it checked by your veterinarian—it might be a tumor. Check the legs for full range of motion, moving them slowly and gently in full range. There should be no clicks or pops.

- **Skin and coat:** Check for sores, bald patches or redness to the skin. The skin should not be dry or flaky. If there are dark grains through the fur that turn red when wet, your dog has fleas.

- **Tail:** The tail should be healthy-looking and not hanging limp. If your dog has been chewing on it, have your vet check it out.

- **Sexual organs:** You should see no discharge from the vagina or penis. (In intact female dogs, a discharge is normal during estrus, but not at other times.)

TAKING YOUR DOG'S TEMPERATURE

Occasionally your vet may ask you to take your dog's temperature. You do this with an ordinary digital rectal thermometer. (Buy a separate one for your dog!) Wash the thermometer with soapy water and sterilize it with isopropyl alcohol. Use petroleum jelly as a lubricant and gently insert the thermometer into your dog's rectum. Hold your dog quietly for about two minutes to obtain a reading. Do not allow your dog to sit down or she might break the thermometer or push it farther into the rectum. Normal temperatures for dogs are 100.5°F to 102°F.

There are also ear thermometer for dogs, similar to the electronic ear thermometers made for people, but they are specially made for dogs.

GIVING MEDICATIONS

If your dog gets sick, she may need medicine. It's important to give your dog all the medicine your vet prescribes, and to follow directions carefully.

The most frequently prescribed type of medication is pills, but occasionally you may have to give liquids. It helps if your dog is comfortable with you handling her mouth. Start at an early age to get her used to you touching her mouth. (Brushing her teeth is an ideal time for this.) Once your dog is used to you touching her mouth, giving medications is less stressful.

Pills

People seem to have a hard time giving pills to pets. The truth is, practice makes perfect. Most dogs will readily swallow a pill if you open their mouth, pop the pill into the back of the mouth and close their jaws with their head tilted upward. Stroking the underside of the throat helps to encourage the dog to swallow. Some pet owners use a little device called a pet piller. It does the same thing, only a little more accurately, so if your aim to the back of the throat is lousy, try one of these.

If you can't get the hang of this, try peanut butter. (Before you bury a pill in peanut butter or any treat, ask your vet if it is okay to administer the medication with food.) Most dogs love peanut butter, it sticks to the roof of their mouth—which provides hours of entertainment for you, and gets the pill down without a fuss. An alternative is to hide the pill in a piece of hot dog (do they even taste it?) or some other treat. If the pill can be ground up (some can't—check with your vet), try mixing it with one of your dog's meals.

Liquid Medications

Liquid medications are fairly easy to administer. Ask your vet for an oral syringe (it looks like a regular syringe with the needle removed) with the amount marked on the syringe in permanent marker. Fill the syringe with the medication, then pull your dog's lower lip out, near where it joins the upper lip, to form a pouch. Squirt the medication gently into the pouch, release it and tilt your dog's head back.

Eye Ointment

Eye ointment usually comes in tubes. Depending how big your dog is, you may need two people to do this. Have someone hold your dog's head gently. Pull down the lower eyelid and expose the eyelid's underside. Squeeze the prescribed amount of ointment in the eyelid's underside and release. Do the same for the other eye, if required.

CHAPTER 19

• •

HEALTH AND YOUR MUTT

When people talk about mutts and health, you may hear them use the phrase *hybrid vigor*. Gregor Mendel coined that term when he crossed plants of two different strains and ended up with a hardier plant. The idea is that the wider and more varied the gene pool, the less likely it is that genetic problems will manifest themselves. But are mutts really healthier than purebred dogs?

ARE MUTTS HEALTHIER?

The answer is a qualified maybe. Since no one keeps overall statistics on the incidence of genetic diseases in mutts versus purebreds, people can make many claims that are based on their own observations. But they can't say anything for sure.

Naturally, I'm going to give you my own observations. I've noticed that as more and more mutts are spayed and neutered, there are fewer dogs with multiple breeds in them and more crossbreeds between two purebreds. These crossbreed dogs generally come from purebred parents who have not been screened for genetic diseases and defects.

Many purebreds have the same or similar diseases, such as hip dysplasia, elbow dysplasia and eye diseases. In many cases, the diseases are caused by the same sets of genes from breed to breed. This means if you cross dogs of two different breeds, but both have the gene for hip dysplasia, you will get a mutt with hip dysplasia. So mixed breeds are *not* immune to genetic diseases.

I have owned several dozen mixed breed dogs in my life. Some came from the animal shelter, others were found on the street, others came from accidental breedings (not mine!), and still others were Alaskan Huskies who were not related. Among these many mutts, I have had dogs with Cushing's disease, hip dysplasia, elbow dysplasia, megaesophagus, epilepsy, zinc responsive dermatosis, autoimmune problems, cataracts and hypothyroid—all diseases with a genetic component.

The diseases I saw in my dogs tend to appear in certain breeds of dogs (the Northern breeds) that were clearly part of the mix in many of my mutts. While this is simply anecdotal evidence, it does clearly show that mutts do indeed get hereditary diseases.

Does this mean mutts have as many health problems as purebred dogs? We don't have adequate statistics, so we really don't know. It's a safe guess that because most mixed breed dogs aren't genetically screened, there will be a certain percentage of mutts with hereditary diseases. We just don't know the percentage. If you know the breeds in your dog's ancestry, it will help you learn what diseases your dog could have.

HEREDITARY AND CONGENITAL DISEASES

What hereditary and congenital diseases might your mutt have? Most mutts are a mixture of purebreds—those same purebreds that suffer from diseases such as hip dysplasia, progressive retinal atrophy, hypothyroidism, elbow dysplasia, epilepsy and Von Willebrand's disease (a type of hemophilia). The purebreds that have those diseases may pass on those problems to the mixes.

Because most mixed breeds are accidents, there's little chance of knowing whether or not a puppy has any hereditary diseases until they manifest themselves. Even adult dogs may have hidden conditions. This is why it is very important to have your dog or puppy checked by a veterinarian when you adopt him.

The following is a listing of common genetic diseases in dogs. This is not a complete list—that would fill a book larger than this one. If your dog is of two or more identifiable breeds, you should probably check breed books to find out what specific genetic diseases are common in those breeds.

Bloat, a Life-Threatening Condition

Bloat (also called gastric dilatation) is a severe, life-threatening condition. It affects many large, deep-chested breeds and may also affect mixed breed dogs; structure seems to be the main factor determining whether the dog will bloat.

Bloat sounds like a case of bad indigestion, but it's much, much more serious. The dog's stomach fills with gas and fluid. As it fills, it begins to twist. This damages the stomach, esophagus and intestines and shuts off the blood supply to those organs. When the stomach twists, the condition then is called gastric torsion or gastric dilatation-volvulus (GDV). If it's not treated, the dog will go into shock and will die a painful death.

Bloat occurs up to three hours after eating. The dog will look pregnant or fat. He may pace back and forth and look uncomfortable. He may drool and attempt to vomit without success. If your dog shows these symptoms after eating, don't attempt to treat him yourself! Get him to the vet as soon as possible.

Older dogs are more susceptible to bloat than dogs younger than three years old. Male dogs will bloat more often than female dogs. Dogs who gulp their food down seem to show some tendency toward bloat, and large, deep-chested dogs seem to be most predisposed.

You can help prevent bloat in your dog. Feed several smaller meals to your dog rather than one or two big meals. Keep your dog's diet consistent so that he doesn't have stomach upsets. Don't feed him and go out; watch your dog for signs of bloat for several hours after feeding. Don't exercise your dog after he has eaten. Encourage slower eating. Some people have gone as far as to put fist-size stones (too big for their dog to swallow) in their dogs' bowls to encourage them to slow down. And finally, don't allow garbage raids, counter raids or other snacking—intentional or unintentional.

Elbow Dysplasia and Osteochondritis Dissecans

Elbow dysplasia is a hereditary disease in which the elbow joints are malformed. Surgery, anti-inflammatory drugs and nutraceuticals (nutritional supplements intended to help mitigate a disease) are recommended treatments for elbow dysplasia. Obviously, surgery can be very expensive and arthritis usually sets in to the joints, further complicating matters.

Osteochondrosis dissecans (OCD) is a condition in which the cartilage thickens in joint areas. This thickened cartilage is more prone to damage and may tear and form a flap or rejoin to the bone. OCD may appear in several joints or only one. If your dog has this condition, he may limp after exercising, suggesting that perhaps this is an injury. However, OCD will cause persistent lameness. You may feel the joint pop or crackle as you examine it. Its onset is usually between four and eight months of age.

If your dog is diagnosed with OCD, your veterinarian may recommend that you rest your dog for several weeks. OCD can be very painful, causing a cartilage flap to form over the elbow. That flap may tear or reattach, and requires surgery to have it removed. Although OCD can be due to trauma, when it is paired with elbow dysplasia, it is most likely due to heredity.

Epilepsy

Epilepsy exists in all breeds and breed mixes. It is usually hereditary in dogs and is quite prevalent in some lines. Studies show some breeds have a genetic predisposition to epilepsy. Idiopathic epilepsy (epilepsy where the specific cause is not known) in dogs is very similar to epilepsy in humans. However, other causes of epilepsy must be ruled out before declaring the condition to be idiopathic. This includes head trauma, poisoning, tick paralysis, parasites, vitamin deficiencies, overheating, intestinal obstructions, liver problems and calcium imbalances.

There are two types of seizures: petit mal and grand mal. Petit mal are usually of short duration, where the dog has a sudden twitch or briefly blanks out. Grand mal seizures are usually spastic seizures that last for several seconds or minutes. The dog may shake, urinate and defecate uncontrollably, and whimper and groan involuntarily. It is very distressing to see a dog have a seizure, but the best thing to do is wait it out and just make sure the dog does not injure himself.

If your dog is epileptic, your vet must rule out various physical causes. If the seizures are frequent or become worse, your vet usually will prescribe a medication to help control them.

Eye Diseases

Mixed breeds are susceptible to hereditary and congenital eye diseases, just like their purebred counterparts. A veterinary ophthalmologist can determine whether your dog has an eye disease. I've listed the most common genetic eye diseases, but there are many others.

Cataracts

A common eye disease in dogs, cataracts are cloudiness of the lens of the eye. The lens may have a small dot or may become opaque, causing complete blindness. Cataracts can be due to either hereditary or environmental conditions.

Many dogs get cataracts as they grow old. However, there is a form of juvenile cataracts that can lead to blindness. Juvenile cataracts are usually hereditary.

Progressive Retinal Atrophy and Central Progressive Retinal Atrophy

Progressive retinal atrophy (PRA) and central progressive retinal atrophy (CPRA) are two eye diseases that lead to blindness. Both are degenerative diseases that may start as early as four to six months of age, or may appear several years later. In both PRA and CPR, the retina degenerates. The dog may first show night blindness before his eyesight deteriorates entirely. There is no cure for these diseases.

Most times the gene that causes these diseases is recessive (which means both parents must have it in order to pass it on), but in certain breeds CPRA can be a dominant gene (which means only one affected parent is needed to pass it on).

Glaucoma

Glaucoma is a painful condition that leads to blindness in dogs. The eye overproduces fluid and intense pressure builds up inside the eyeball. Some forms of glaucoma are due to injury and other conditions, but some forms are inherited. Glaucoma may require the removal of the entire eye.

Heart Problems

Dogs suffer from a variety of heart conditions, both congenital and hereditary. They can range from extreme, such as a severe heart defect that will lead to death, to minor, such as a slight heart murmur. Your veterinarian may be able to diagnose certain heart conditions by listening with a stethoscope, but some heart diseases may need complex machinery and a cardiologist to diagnose.

One of my Alaskan Huskies had an undetected heart condition for years, even though many veterinarians had listened to his heart. He showed promise, but would not run as far as he needed to. After several years, I chose to retire him because I thought he simply didn't like to run. Later in his life, I saw the signs of congenital heart failure. The veterinarian who examined him noted the marked heart murmur no one else had detected in all those years. The murmur had been too small for the other veterinarians to detect, but clearly was a problem for my dog.

Congenital Heart Disease

Congenital heart disease is present at birth. Malformations of the heart or great vessels surrounding the heart all fall into this category. Congenital heart conditions may get worse as a dog grows up. No one knows if these heart defects are hereditary, but many believe that they are. They can be mild or serious—anything from a heart murmur to life-threatening abnormalities.

Subaortic Stenosis

Subaortic stenosis (SAS) is an insidious hereditary condition that may show no outward signs. Then, an apparently healthy dog suddenly drops over dead. SAS is a narrowing of the outflow of the left ventricle (called a stenosis) just below the aortic valve. The heart must work harder to push more blood through the narrow opening, causing problems.

SAS can be difficult to diagnose. The heart murmur, a common symptom of SAS, may be difficult to detect. The dog may also have arrhythmias (irregular heartbeat). A veterinary cardiologist can diagnose SAS through either Doppler echocardiography or cardiac catheterization. The prognosis for a long, healthy life is poor.

Hip Dysplasia

Hip dysplasia is a crippling genetic disease caused by the malformation of the hip socket. No amount of good nutrition and care will stop it. Almost every breed has some incidence of hip dysplasia, so it's also likely to turn up in mutts—even small ones. (You may hear people say small dogs do not have hip dysplasia, but the Bulldog and the Pug have the highest incidence of hip dysplasia among purebreds, according to the Orthopedic Foundation for Animals.)

In mild cases, your vet may be able to help mitigate the effects with nutraceuticals such as glucosamine, chondroitin and creatine, and anti-inflammatories such as aspirin, Metacam, Rimadyl, Zubrin or Dermamaxx. Some cases are so bad that the dog must have surgery. In some extreme cases, the dog must be euthanized. Surgery is extremely expensive—thousands of dollars in most cases.

Hypothyroidism

Hypothyroidism occurs when the dog's thyroid gland produces insufficient thyroid hormone. Symptoms can include lethargy, dull and dry coat, obesity or weight gain, and a thinning coat. The dog may seek warmer areas. Some dogs just seem slow and dull, when really they are suffering from hypothyroidism.

Some forms of hypothyroidism may be hereditary. Your vet can diagnose hypothyroidism through a blood test. If your dog is suffering from hypothyroidism, your veterinarian may prescribe a form of synthetic thyroid hormone. Dogs on hormone therapy do quite well.

Von Willebrand's Disease

Von Willebrand's disease (VWD) is a type of bleeding disorder. In most cases the bleeding is mild, and it lessens with age, but there have been severe cases. Prolonged nosebleeds, bleeding under the skin, blood in the stool and urine and bleeding from the gums after tooth eruptions are all signs of the disease.

There are two types of Von Willebrand's disease: inherited and acquired. The acquired form of Von Willebrand's is related familial autoimmune thyroid disease. Your veterinarian can diagnose VWD with a blood test.

INTERNAL PARASITES

There is a variety of internal parasites that can afflict dogs. Worms and other internal parasites can damage your dog's health, and some can even be transferred to you. It's very important to eliminate these pests if you want to keep your dog healthy.

If you suspect your dog has worms, you might be tempted to treat him with over-the-counter dewormers. Different worms require different treatments, though, so unless you have experience with recognizing worms, treating your dog with an all-purpose dewormer is not a good idea. Not all dewormers work on all worms, and some that say they are good for certain kinds of worms may not work well or may have adverse side effects. All dewormers are poisons, and even those with a relatively high margin of safety can make your dog sick. That's why it's best to work with your veterinarian to come up with the best treatment plan.

What kind of internal parasites can your dog get? I've broken them down into three categories: worms that inhabit the gastrointestinal tract, heartworms, and microscopic organisms.

Gastrointestinal Worms

When we say that a dog has "worms," we're usually talking about the worms that inhabit the gastrointestinal tract. These include roundworms (*Toxocara canis*), hookworms (*Ancylostoma caninum*), tapeworms (*Dipylidium caninum*) and whipworms (*Trichuris vulpis*).

With the exception of hookworms, most worms enter the dog via an oral-fecal transmission route (the dog eats something contaminated with fecal material that has worm eggs in it). Roundworms may also be transferred from mother to puppies before they're born, or through the mother's milk. Tapeworms may also be picked up by swallowing fleas or eating road kill, rodents or raw game. Hookworm infestation occurs through skin penetration or is passed to a puppy through his mother's milk.

Of all the worms, roundworms are the most common. Roundworm, hookworm and whipworm infestations can kill puppies and dogs, so it is important to have your vet perform a fecal exam on your dog. Both roundworms and tapeworms can be transmitted to humans.

Heartworm

Heartworm is an internal parasite that is transmitted by mosquitoes. It can kill your dog. Most states within the continental United States have heartworm, although it is less prevalent in the Western states.

Mosquitoes transmit heartworm by feeding on an infected dog. The *microfilariae* (heartworm larvae) from the infected dog incubate within the mosquito for several days. When the infected mosquito bites another dog, it injects the infectious microfilariae into the dog and that dog becomes infected with heartworm.

Heartworm is very easy to prevent with medication, but very difficult to treat once a dog has it. In many areas, heartworm is seasonal and you only have to administer the preventive medication during the spring and summer months. Heartworm season is year-round in the Southern states and areas where the temperatures seldom reach freezing.

Because the heartworm preventive medication can actually harm a dog with the heartworm infection, your veterinarian should administer a heartworm test before putting your dog on a preventive. It is a simple blood test that screens for the presence of microfilariae.

There are several heartworm preventives available, including some that help control other parasites. Most veterinarians now prescribe monthly heartworm preventives, although there are still a few daily preventives available. Do not use the daily preventives, because they are less effective if administered incorrectly. There's now a six-month injectable, Proheart 6 (moxidectin), that also prevents heartworm. It is given as an injection and can only be administered by your vet.

The monthly heartworm preventives include:

- **Heartgard (ivermectin):** Heartgard Plus has pyrantel pamoate and also controls roundworms and hookworms. Some dogs are sensitive to ivermectin, but this sensitivity is rare.
- **Interceptor (milbemycin) and Sentinel (milbemycin and lufenuron):** Interceptor controls heartworm as well as hookworms, roundworms and whipworms. Sentinel also controls fleas.
- **Revolution (selamectin):** A topical application, Revolution prevents heartworm and fleas.

Microscopic Parasites

Don't drink the water! We've heard that warning before. Certain microorganisms can ruin your vacation, and dogs can get them too. The most common are giardia and coccidia.

Giardia is a microscopic organism that can cause extreme diarrhea and vomiting. It can be chronic and may reoccur even after treatment. Only your vet can prescribe medications that will cure giardia.

Dogs can pick up *Giardia* by drinking water from streams and lakes or other contaminated sources. I knew someone whose dog who contracted giardiasis after eating bird poop! You can contract giardiasis from the same water source or if you don't wash your hands after cleaning up after your infected dog. Giardiasis symptoms can be mild to extreme.

Coccidia are microscopic parasites that frequently affect puppies in crowded puppy mill conditions. Occasionally puppies from reputable breeders may contract coccidia if an infected dog comes in contact with the puppies. Your veterinarian can prescribe medication to treat coccidia.

EXTERNAL PARASITES

Scratch! Scratch! External parasites can be intolerable. Fleas, ticks and mites can cause misery to an otherwise happy, healthy dog. But more than just making your dog miserable, external parasites can cause severe health problems and, in certain instances, carry dangerous diseases to you and your family.

Fleas

Fleas are nasty little bloodsuckers who carry fearsome diseases such as bubonic plague, tapeworm and other diseases. While canines tend to have a high resistance to plague, you don't, so treat these critters like the serious danger they are.

Fleas flourish everywhere except places that are very cold, very dry or at high altitudes. I live in such a place (in the Rocky Mountains) and have few problems with fleas, but those fleas we do see tend to carry plague. So fleas are a problem wherever you go.

If you suspect a flea infestation, search for fleas on your dog, especially around his belly and groin area, at the base of his tail and around his ears. A common sign of fleas are deposits of black flea feces that look like grains of pepper and turn red when wet. Of course, seeing the little suckers jump is a sure sign of flea infestation.

Tick collars work well, but flea collars seldom work because of the large area they must cover. Poor Lucky!

If you find fleas on your dog, you have a flea infestation in your home. So how do you declare war on fleas? Talk to your veterinarian about ways to combat the problem. Often your veterinarian can recommend a system that will fight fleas in the yard, in your home and on your dog. Your vet will recommend products based on your climate and your dog's age and health, and will also recommend products that are safe to use together. Be very careful about mixing products, and always read the label.

You'll have to vacuum all carpets and furniture—anywhere fleas hide. Some people put a piece of flea collar in the vacuum cleaner bag to kill the fleas.

New systemic treatments (see the box on page 176) have made most drastic measures (flea bombs and the like) obsolete, except for the worst infestations.

FLEA SYSTEMICS

Systemic treatments work inside your dog's system to kill fleas. Some are pills and some are spot-ons that you put on the back of the dog's neck. Generally (but not always), systemics are non-toxic to mammals, but they do a great job on fleas. Some of the products available include:

- Frontline (fipronil) and Frontline Plus (fipronil and metho-prene) kill fleas within 24 to 48 hours. Frontline Plus contains an insect growth regulator that keeps immature fleas from reproducing. This spot-on is effective for three months against adult fleas and one month against ticks.

- Advantage (imidacloprid) works by killing both adult fleas and larvae within 48 hours. This spot-on is effective for six weeks against fleas.

- Program (lufenuron) works by preventing flea eggs from hatching or maturing into adults. It is a monthly pill.

- Biospot (pyrethrins and fenoxycarb) has an insect growth regulator that keeps immature fleas from reproducing. This spot-on kills fleas and ticks for one month. I've also seen it repel flies.

Ticks

Ticks are bloodsucking relatives of the spider and carry a host of dangerous diseases, including Rocky Mountain spotted fever, ehrlichiosis, babesiosis and the much-publicized Lyme disease. These diseases can seriously damage your dog's health and may even be fatal in extreme cases. Your vet can test for tick-borne diseases with a blood test and can treat them with various medications.

If your dog tests positive for one of these tick-borne diseases, consider having your own doctor test you for the same disease. Ticks can transmit these same diseases to humans and, in rare instances, contact with your dog's bodily fluids may also pass these diseases to you.

When should you suspect your dog has one of these tick-borne diseases?

- **Babesiosis:** Common signs are fever, lethargy and lack of appetite.
- **Canine ehrlichiosis:** Common signs are fever, discharge from the eyes and nose, and swollen limbs (edema). A dog with

canine ehrlichiosis may lack appetite, be unusually tired and have swollen lymph nodes.

- **Lyme disease:** Common signs are lameness and fever. A dog with Lyme disease may lack appetite, be unusually tired and have swollen lymph nodes. The dog may also have bouts of unexplained lameness that can become chronic.

- **Rocky Mountain spotted fever:** Common signs are high fever, abdominal pain, coughing, lack of appetite, lethargy, swelling of the face or limbs, depression, vomiting, diarrhea and muscle or joint pain.

In some places, ticks are so prevalent that you must check your dog after each time he has been outside. In other places, you may need to check your dog only when he has been walking through tall grasses or brush.

If you find a tick on your dog, avoid handling it or you risk exposing yourself to disease. Instead, treat the area with a good tick insecticide approved for use on dogs, wait a few minutes, then try to remove it. Wear latex gloves and use tweezers. Firmly grasp the tick with the tweezers as close to the skin as possible and gently pull. Don't try to pull the tick out if it resists—you may end up leaving portions of the tick embedded in your dog, and the area can become infected. Wait for the tick to drop off and then dispose of it in a sealed container.

A Mite Is a Teeny Spider

Actually, mites are small arachnids and so are relatives of spiders and ticks. Your vet can take a skin scraping to determine what type of mites you dog has and how to treat them. When mites get out of control, they cause a skin condition called mange. There are three major types of mites:

1. **Ear mites** (*Otodectes cynotis*) often look like reddish-brown earwax in your dog's ears. Your dog may scratch or shake his head frequently. Don't try to treat ear mites with over-the-counter solutions because there may already be a secondary infection. Your vet will need to clean out the reddish-brown gunk and then will give you ear drops to kill the mites and handle any infections.

2. **Demodectic mites** (*Demodex canis*) feed primarily on the cells of hair follicles. And infestation appears as dry, scaly, red skin,

with hair loss, mostly around the face. Demodectic mites live on all dogs, but the skin condition known as demodectic mange is thought to be triggered by an impaired immune system. Most of the time, localized demodectic mange clears up on its own. If it is generalized (all over the dog's body) or doesn't clear up, it can be difficult to treat.

3. **Sarcoptic mites** (*Sarcoptes scabei*) are highly contagious. This type of mange may spread quickly in kennels. It is itchy with hair loss and a red rash. The dog may have ugly sores from scratching. Your vet can prescribe a topical product to treat sarcoptic mange. Your dog may need to be treated with medicated baths and body dips. If the sores are infected, your vet may prescribe antibiotics.

ALLERGIES

Allergies and intolerances seem to be occurring more frequently among dogs. Perhaps it's the pollutants in today's environment or perhaps it's indiscriminate breeding (allergies do have a genetic component), or perhaps it's something we don't yet understand.

When we think of allergies, we might think of the sitcom version of a person sneezing all the time—and certainly, some allergic dogs do sneeze. But many allergies may appear as food allergies or contact allergies, which cause skin irritations. Dogs can even be allergic to fleas.

Food Allergies

Food allergies are becoming increasingly common among dogs. They're a bit tricky to diagnose. Your vet will recommend a hypoallergenic diet for several weeks. This diet usually has a novel protein source; that is, a protein source that dogs generally don't eat, such as fish or venison. (Contrary to popular belief, lamb is *not* a hypoallergenic meat.) The diet may have an unusual carbohydrate source too, such as potatoes or barley. After your dog is on this diet for several weeks, you add the potentially problem ingredients, one by one, to see which one triggers the allergic reaction. Some dog owners are so relieved to have their dogs free from the allergy that they keep them on the hypoallergenic diet for life.

External Allergies

Contact allergies occur when the dog comes in contact with something external to his body that triggers an allergic reaction. Some contact

ALLERGY OR INTOLERANCE?

Dogs who are *allergic* to certain foods will show their allergies in the form of rashes, poor coat and other conditions. Dogs who are *intolerant* of a certain food will not be able to digest the food. For example, dogs typically are lactose-intolerant, meaning they can't break down the sugars in milk. This often results in diarrhea and gastric upsets when they eat milk products. Dogs who are allergic to certain foods (beef, for example) may be able to digest the food just fine, but the problems manifest themselves in the skin and coat.

allergies are apparent; some aren't as easy to diagnose. For example, if your dog's skin looks irritated and is itchy after using a particular shampoo, it's likely the dog is allergic to a chemical in that shampoo. However, you might not know why your dog's nose and face are swollen and irritated. Many dogs are allergic to plastic or rubber, and may react to the plastic bowls you use to feed them. Most contact allergies are diagnosed based on the owner's observations.

Flea Bite Dermatitis

A dog with flea bite dermatitis is allergic to flea saliva. Flea bite dermatitis can cause itchy skin and hot spots, and can drive your dog crazy. Eliminating fleas from your mutt and your home will solve the problem and provide welcome relief. Your veterinarian can prescribe medications to alleviate the itching.

WHAT ELSE CAN GO WRONG?

It's a longer list than I can handle in this chapter, or even in this book, Puppies, especially, are mischievous litter critters, and can get into all sorts of trouble—some of it health-related. I'll discuss some of the more common but relatively minor canine health problems in this chapter, and look at canine emergencies in Chapter 20.

Broken Nails

Your dog may break or crack a nail, especially if you let the nails grow too long. If the nail has broken beyond the quick and there is no bleeding, simply trim the nail and file off any rough edges. If the nail is bleeding, you can stop the bleeding with styptic powder, silver nitrate or an electric nail cauterizer available through pet mail order catalogs (in a pinch, you can also use cornstarch). You can then paint the nail with a skin bonding agent, available from your veterinarian or through veterinary supply houses.

Diarrhea

Changes in diet, overeating, unfamiliar water and nervousness can cause diarrhea, but so can parvovirus, internal parasites, rancid food, allergies and other serious ailments. If your dog is dehydrated (see the box below), has a fever (over 102°F), or has extreme or bloody diarrhea, take him to your veterinarian as soon as possible.

If your dog has mild diarrhea (soft stools, but not liquid and without mucus), is not dehydrated and is not vomiting, you can give him one tablespoon of a kaolin product (such as Kaopectate) or a bismuth subsalicylate product (such as Pepto-Bismol). Withhold your dog's next meal to see if the diarrhea improves. Encourage your dog to drink water or an unflavored pediatric electrolyte solution. If there is no diarrhea or vomiting, you can feed the dog a mixture of boiled hamburger and rice. If your mutt's condition does not improve or becomes worse, contact your veterinarian.

IS YOUR DOG DEHYDRATED?

Dehydration can occur in any season, summer or winter. To determine if your dog is dehydrated, do a simple skin-snap test. Gently use your thumb and forefinger to pull up on the skin just above the shoulder blades. It should snap back when you release it. If it melts back slowly, or worse, stays there, your dog should be treated for dehydration. (It's a good idea to try this test when your dog isn't dehydrated, because many factors, such as breed and age, can affect the results. If you know what's normal for your dog, you will also know what's abnormal.)

Another place to check is your dog's mouth and lips. If your dog's gums are sticky, not moist, he's dehydrated. You can also perform a skin-snap test on his jowls.

To treat for dehydration, give your dog water on unflavored pediatric electrolytes (available in the baby section of the grocery store). If the dehydration is extreme or is combined with heatstroke, seek *immediate* veterinary attention.

Vomiting

Dogs vomit for a variety of reasons. They will sometimes eat grass and vomit. They also vomit due to obstructions, enlarged esophagus, parvovirus and other serious illnesses, allergies and rancid food. If your mutt vomits more than once or twice, projectile vomits, starts becoming dehydrated, has severe diarrhea along with vomiting, has a fever (over 102°F) or retches without vomiting, take him to the veterinarian immediately.

Foxtails

Foxtails, or grass awns, are seeds from grasslike plants. They have a sharp, burrowing head with a tail that looks like a fox's tail (hence the name). These seeds have a nasty habit of getting into your dog's coat and ears. With each movement, they burrow further into the dog's skin.

Check your dog thoroughly after he's been outside for burrs and foxtails. Check his ears, too. I've seen foxtails bury themselves deep into a dog's skin. They can cause abscesses and can even enter internal organs.

Itchy Skin and Hot Spots

Your mutt could have itchy skin for a number of reasons. If your dog's coat is dull and dry, try adding one to two teaspoons of canola oil to his food once a day and a hard-boiled egg three times a week. If your mutt's coat remains dry and brittle or thin, consider having him tested for hypothyroidism.

Some dogs are allergic to certain ingredients in their foods, which can cause skin problems (see page 178). Your veterinarian can prescribe a special hypoallergenic diet.

Hot spots are areas of moist dermatitis (skin inflammation) that may become infected. The symptoms are reddening skin, missing hair and oozing, woundlike lesions. Allergies, matted fur or some other form of irritation frequently causes them.

Shave or clip all hair surrounding the hot spot and clean twice daily with a solution of 10 percent betadine and 90 percent water. If the hot spots are too painful, infected or extensive, your veterinarian may have to anesthetize your dog to shave the areas and then prescribe corticosteroids and antibiotics.

Lumps and Bumps on the Skin

Most lumps are benign. You can determine whether or not the lump is normal by checking the same place on the opposite side of the dog.

Usually lumps that appear on both sides of the dog in the same place are normal.

Show any suspicious lump or bump to your veterinarian. Lumps that are oozing, red, dark, irregular in size and shape or swift-growing may be very serious. If your female dog has lumps on her mammary glands, they may be cancerous mammary tumors that require surgery. A large, doughy lump on the stomach might be a hernia that your veterinarian may have to fix.

Rapidly growing lumps may be a form of abscess or infection. Abscesses occur when foreign bodies (such as foxtails) enter the skin, or when a wound closes with bacteria inside. Abscesses are serious. Your veterinarian must drain the abscess and prescribe antibiotics. Do not attempt to drain the abscess yourself or the wound may become even more infected.

Incontinence

Incontinence is generally a sign of a more serious problem, such as a bladder or urinary tract infection or bladder stones. Have your vet examine your dog to determine the cause of incontinence. Occasionally, spayed female dogs dribble when they get older, and may need medication to correct this.

If your dog crouches down and urinates when you yell at him or touch him, it may be a form of submissive urination. This is a sign that he respects your authority and is being submissive. Some dogs are more submissive than others. Scolding or yelling at your dog will only aggravate the problem. You can stop this behavior by remaining calm and speaking quietly. Pet your dog under the chin gently and don't act angry. Most dogs who are overly submissive may require some gentle confidence builders, such as training using positive-reinforcement techniques.

Paneosteitis

Paneosteitis, or pano, is a condition in which a growing puppy suddenly becomes lame. This lameness may be mild to severe, and may affect different limbs at different times. The onset of pano is somewhere around five to 12 months and usually affects males more than females. Large and giant breeds are more often affected by pano. It may have a genetic component.

If your puppy has pano, your veterinarian may prescribe analgesics and rest. He may ask you to limit the pup's exercise. Eventually, as the puppy gets older, the pain subsides and the puppy grows out of it.

Skunks

It doesn't get much worse than being skunked. But before you go and buy out the local supermarket's stock of tomato juice, save your money. You'll just end up with a stinky, pink dog.

Instead, buy a good commercial skunk-odor remover or use the do-it-yourself baking soda and hydrogen peroxide recipe described below.

I've never used a commercial skunk-odor remover, so I can't vouch for their effectiveness. However, I had the most unfortunate luck of having one of my dogs get skunked while he was playing in our back-yard. The skunk decided to spray the dog from the other side of the fence. I decided to try the following recipe for getting rid of skunk odor. I found it works extremely well. My dog came out smelling bet-ter than he had before he got skunked.

You can double the recipe with ease, if your dog is big or if he is particularly stinky.

- 1/2 quart hydrogen peroxide
- 1/8 cup baking soda
- 1 teaspoon shampoo or liquid soap

Wash the dog with this and rinse thoroughly. Don't get any in your dog's eyes. Don't save any of it in a container—it might explode.

CHAPTER 20

EMERGENCIES AND DISASTERS

Emergencies are not just about health. You must be prepared not only for injuries and severe illnesses, but also for disasters. Wildfires, floods, tornados, hurricanes and even terrorist attacks are all potential disasters we face in the modern world. Your dog is relying on you to keep her healthy and safe. The main thing is not to panic. Your dog needs you to remain levelheaded and calm in any emergency.

PREPARING FOR THE WORST

Emergencies and disasters never happen at convenient times. But you can be ready if you plan for them.

So how do you prepare for not only the occasional emergency, but also a potential disaster? As the Boy Scouts of America say, "Be Prepared." Plan your strategy now before trouble hits.

Where Will You Stay?

For most of us with pets, leaving our best friends behind is unthinkable. But most disaster shelters set up by the American Red Cross won't take pets (although they do accept service dogs). Where will you stay if you have to leave your home and take your pets with you?

I recommend that you locate friends or family out of the potential disaster area who will take you and your pets. Talk to them now. Don't assume they *will* take you and your pets and then find out later they won't! This happened to me! Ask *now* before you're forced into a bad situation.

If you don't have family or friends where you can stay, have a list of hotels and motels within a certain radius of your house (five miles, 10 miles, 25 miles, 50 miles) that will allow pets. Locate kennels that are outside the potential disaster area, in case you must stay in a place that doesn't allow pets.

Although I don't recommend it, a last resort can be to contact animal shelters and find out if they can care for your pets in an emergency. The reason I don't recommend it is that in a disaster, shelters are frequently crowded and usually have pets who have been lost or displaced.

Some animal shelters and foster programs can sometimes take pets in during an emergency, but they should be your last resort. (This is an Akita mix at a shelter.)

THE LATEST INFORMATION

I have been through two forest fires: one that forced us to evacuate and one that put us on standby evacuation. In both instances, I found that no matter how good the media are, there is going to be a time lag between when things happen and when they tell you about them—and possibly faulty information.

Two things worth having are a computer with an Internet connection and a police/fire emergency scanner. In huge disasters, assuming the phone lines and power still work, authorities will often post the latest news and information to dedicated web sites.

In the last big fire, I was able to get up-to-date information via the National Forest Service's Web site. The police and fire scanner gave me information on how far the fire was from my house and whether it was out of control and/or heading in my direction.

Preparing for the Big One

Sometimes you have several days of advance warning, such as when a hurricane comes or with some large wildfires. Other times, you have little or no warning whatsoever, such as a house fire or a tornado. Have an emergency kit ready to grab and go before disaster strikes. In this emergency kit, you should have the following items:

- Pet first-aid kit (see page 192)
- Enough pet food and potable water for three days
- Copies of your pet's health records and vaccination records
- Photos of your pet in case she gets lost
- Bowls, leashes and a can opener
- Travel crate
- Contact information for hotels, motels, emergency veterinarians, your veterinarian and other numbers you might need

ID, Please

Your dog should have two forms of ID: tags and a permanent form, either a microchip or a tattoo. She needs tags because not everyone knows to look for permanent ID; she needs permanent ID because your dog may lose her collar and tags.

There are pluses and minuses to all forms of identification. Tags, which are the cheapest and easiest, can be removed from the dog or lost. With permanent ID, many people don't know to check for tattoos or microchips. And even if they do, many people don't know how to use the number to track down the dog's owner.

Microchips must be checked with a scanner, so even if a person knew to check for a microchip on a dog, they probably would not have a scanner. And because there is no standard for microchips at this time, some scanners don't read some microchips.

Many animal shelters have scanners (supplied at low cost or free of charge by the microchip manufacturers), but not all of them.

Tags

Tags are a cheap form of identification. Most tags cost between $4 and $8, although very fancy tags can cost between $10 and $20, or even more. Tags are easy to get. Many pet supply stores have tag-engraving machines that cost under $10 and will engrave the tags right there while you wait. Some malls have tag-engraving machines for pet tags or luggage. Your vet probably has mail-in forms at their office and you can also buy tags through pet supply catalogs and online. I've even gotten some tags free with my purchase of pet supplies.

There's no reason your dog should be without tags. Every day, lost dogs turn up at shelters with collars but no tags. Make two tags—one for her to wear now and one as a spare. When you travel or go on vacation, have a separate tag made with your cell phone number and the place where you will be, plus the dates.

What if your dog loses her collar or tags? Luckily, there are two forms of permanent identification that you can have on your dog: a tattoo and microchip.

Tattoos

Tattoos are a visible form of identification permanently marked into the skin. Unlike human tattoos, canine tattoos are not painful, but they can be distressing because the markers buzz loudly. Most dogs hate having it done.

Tattoos are placed either inside the dog's ear or on the inside of the thigh. Inside the ear is a poor choice—dog thieves will lop off an ear to remove the identification.

They are less expensive than microchips. You must choose a unique number for your dog—most people choose their Social Security number. And those numbers must be registered with an ID registry, or else they cannot be used to trace the dog back to you. There have been instances of tattooed dogs who weren't registered with a national registry, and they might as well not have been tattooed.

You can get tattoos done at a veterinary clinic, through a dog club or by a groomer. The major national registries are National Dog Registry and Tattoo-A-Pet (both are listed in Appendix A), and both can refer you to tattooists in your area. Tattoos cost anywhere from $5 to $25, plus the registration fee.

Microchips

Microchips are about the size of a grain of rice and are inserted under the skin, usually between the dog's shoulder blades. Microchips are encased in surgical glass or plastic and are only activated when a scanner is passed over them. You must have a vet implant the chip, but it only takes a few seconds and is a lot like getting an injection. Vets, dog clubs and sometimes, animal shelters provide microchips.

When the scanner is passed over the dog's body, it reads the microchip similar to the way a supermarket scanner reads a bar code. Then, as with a tattoo, the microchip number must be registered and the person with the scanner must know who to call to report the dog's number. Most microchip registries give you a tag with their toll-free hotline to put on the dog's collar (you'll find a list of registries in Appendix A). Microchips cost anywhere from $25 to $50, plus the registration fee.

When the Unthinkable Happens

Disaster strikes and you're not at home. The police and firefighters have barricaded the roads leading to your home. Who's going to evacuate your pets?

Arrange well in advance with a trustworthy neighbor who owns pets for a way to get your dog out. (Offer to do likewise for their pets.) You will have to give them a key so they can enter your home in an emergency. Have a predetermined location to meet. Tell them where the emergency kit is and how to contact you. They should do likewise.

If no one can get to your house except emergency personnel, you might have some luck talking with them and asking them to rescue your dog. Prominently display window stickers (available through pet mail order houses—I received mine free through a dog food company!) alerting emergency personnel that you have pets inside. Sometimes animal control officers will come by to save pets and bring them to nearby shelters.

But what do you do if emergency personnel won't let you back to your house and you know your dog is there and nobody will rescue her? I can't tell you what to do in this circumstance; you'll have to make up your own mind. Yes, I have heard of several people who broke through (or snuck through) police barriers to rescue their pets. They risked their lives doing so; people have died trying to rescue their pets in disasters.

LOST DOG

There's nothing more gut-wrenching than having your dog get lost. Once your dog escapes and you can no longer find her, contact the local animal control department, the local police department, and any veterinarians and shelters in the immediate area. Be very diligent and phone the animal shelters every day, and visit them at least every other day. Many times, shelter personnel have misidentified dogs or failed to notice a missing dog request.

Watch the "Found" ads in the local papers and, if you can, run a "Lost" ad. Give a detailed description—not just "mixed breed." A good description might be:

> LOST!
> Husky-mix, neutered male, 60 lbs, brown face,
> white body with spots.
> Friendly. Answers to "Razor."
> (303) 555-1212.
> Reward.

Post flyers with a photo of your dog and hand them out to all your neighbors and the staff at the local veterinary clinics and animal shelters. Be sure to include a contact number and a photo of the dog, and an accurate description, on the flyer. Visit all your neighbors and don't be shy—someone may have picked up your dog.

Some people put up posts on various Internet e-mail lists about their lost dog, but I'm not sure how effective this is. Many people don't read flyers tacked to signposts, and while there are plenty of good people on the Internet, the vast majority won't ever be in the place where you lost your dog. The USDA has a Web site for people to post lost pets at the missing pet network: www.missingpet.net. This is a free service and is worth checking.

Most people offer a reward, which is fine. But be careful! There are scam artists who will take advantage of your situation and say they have your dog but live outside your area and need money to ship your dog home. If you get a phone call from an individual who thinks they have your dog, try to arrange to have a veterinarian or a local animal shelter confirm that this is your dog. If they aren't too far away, take the time to drive to see the dog to make sure it is your dog. Then you can pay the person their reward and take your dog home.

Many stray dogs are picked up within a few hours of getting out. There are a few who manage to elude capture for several days. Unless they are totally mystified by their surroundings, many dogs are able to find their way back to their owners. If you can stay where you lost your dog for a few days, you should. You might be able to find her when she decides she's hungry and comes looking for you.

HEALTH EMERGENCIES

You need to be prepared for a health emergency all the time, because emergencies are never convenient. Talk with your veterinarian on how to prepare for an emergency. They may recommend including certain items in your dog's emergency first-aid kit that I have not mentioned (see page 192). Ask them to show you how to perform CPR and mouth-to-mouth resuscitation.

Always have the following phone numbers on hand in case of an emergency:

- Your veterinarian's phone number, pager number and after-hours number
- The phone number and directions to the two nearest emergency veterinary clinics
- The phone number of a local or national animal poison control center

How to Muzzle Your Dog

In an emergency, you may have to muzzle your dog. Even the gentlest dog may bite if she's frightened or injured. Have a quick muzzle (sold in pet supply stores and by mail order) available. If you don't have one, you can make a muzzle from a bandage, a rope, a belt, a tie or any long piece of cloth. *Never muzzle a dog who is having problems breathing, is overheated or has a sucking chest wound.*

Take your piece of bandage (or rope or whatever you've found to make into a muzzle). Start in the middle of the bandage and place it underneath the dog's chin. Pull the ends of the bandage upward, tie it across the top of the dog's muzzle, and then bring it back down under the chin and tie it again. Take the two loose ends and tie them behind the dog's head. You want the muzzle to be secure enough that it can't fall off, but still leave room for your dog to breathe without any extra effort.

Broken Bones and Car Accidents

Fractures to the head, chest or back may be life-threatening. Use a stiff board or a large blanket to transport the dog (slide the board under the dog) and seek immediate veterinary attention.

If your dog has broken her leg, you can make a splint from a stick, a rolled-up piece of stiff cardboard or even a rolled-up newspaper. Put the splint alongside the broken leg and wrap either VetWrap or tape around it. Transport your dog to the veterinarian as soon as possible.

Do you know what to do in an emergency? Your dog is depending on you.

ASSEMBLING A FIRST-AID KIT

Having a first-aid kit for your dog is important. It's easy to get the items you'll need:

- Baby aspirin
- Bandage scissors
- Bandage tape
- Betadine solution
- Cortisone cream
- Disposable latex gloves
- An emergency veterinary hospital's phone number
- Hydrogen peroxide
- Kaolin product (Kaopectate)
- Large and small non-stick bandage pads
- Local poison control center phone number
- Mineral oil
- Petroleum jelly (Vaseline)
- Pressure bandages
- Quick muzzle
- Rectal thermometer
- Self-adhesive wrap (VetWrap or Elastoplast)
- Sterile gauze wrappings
- Sterile sponges
- Surgical glue or VetBond (available from veterinary supply catalogs)
- Syrup of ipecac
- Triple antibiotic ointment or nitrofurizone (available from veterinary supply catalogs)
- Tweezers
- Unflavored pediatric electrolyte solution (Pedialyte)
- Your veterinarian's phone number, pager or after-hours number

Burns

A severe burn, where the skin is charred or where underlying tissue is exposed, requires immediate veterinary attention. You can treat minor burns over a small area with ice packs or cold water. Do not use water on extensive burns, or your dog may go into shock. Ice and then aloe vera is a good burn treatment after the burn has blistered.

Choking or Difficulty Breathing

Signs of choking and difficulty breathing include gagging, coughing, wheezing and pale or blue gums and tongue. Do not muzzle your dog. Do loosen your dog's collar and anything else that might restrict breathing. Check your dog's mouth and throat for any object that might be obstructing the airway. If you see something that you can remove with tweezers, do so. Do not use your fingers; you can accidentally push the item farther down. If the item is lodged in the throat, try pushing on the dog's abdomen to expel the object. Seek immediate veterinary attention—even if you manage to dislodge it.

If your dog has stopped breathing, mouth-to-mouth resuscitation may be the only way to save her life. Make sure your dog's airway is clear. Close her mouth, hold her jaws together and blow gently into her nose. Don't blow too hard or you may rupture a lung. Her side should expand, but only as much as if she were breathing. Now let the air leave the lungs. Breathe into the nose again and release. Continue to do this until your dog is breathing on her own.

Ask your veterinarian to demonstrate for you how to perform CPR correctly.

Cuts, Injuries and Dog Bites

You can clean minor cuts and scrapes yourself with a 10 percent betadine–90 percent water solution. Then apply a triple antibiotic ointment and watch for signs of infection. Seek veterinary attention if you see signs of redness or inflammation, or signs of infection such as oozing pus.

Severe cuts and lacerations will most likely require stitches. Use pressure bandages to slow or stop the bleeding, except in severe crushing injuries. If the injuries are severe, such as from a car accident, there may be internal bleeding. Use a stiff board to transport the dog to a veterinary immediately.

In the case of arterial bleeding, the blood is bright red and sprays out with each heartbeat. Use pressure bandages and apply pressure directly to the artery. Seek immediate veterinary attention.

For deep puncture wounds, determine how deep the puncture is. If the object is still embedded, do not remove it; just seek immediate veterinary treatment. If the puncture is a dog bite that is not serious, you can clean the wound with a betadine and water solution. Your veterinarian might want to prescribe antibiotics to prevent infection. Be sure that both your dog and the biting dog are current with their rabies vaccinations.

Cut pads tend to bleed badly. Staunch the bleeding with styptic powder and then apply an antibiotic. You can wrap the foot with gauze and put a bootie on, such as the winter boots you can buy at a pet supply store or from a sled dog outfitter. (Booties.com is one source.) If the cut or split is minor, you can take a piece of leather cut a little larger than the cut on the pad and stick it to the dog's pad using surgical or super glue. This will help the pad heal.

Electrocution

If your dog is still in contact with the source of electricity, *do not* touch your dog or you might also be shocked. Use a wooden broom handle or other non-conductive item to unplug the cord or to move your dog. Keep the dog warm and seek emergency veterinary treatment. Administer mouth-to-mouth resuscitation as described in "Difficulty Breathing" on page 193.

Fishhooks

If your dog has stepped on a fishhook or has one in her mouth, take her to a vet. If no vet is available, you may have to muzzle your dog and look for where the barb of the hook is. Push the barb forward through the skin, if necessary, to expose it, and then snip it off with a pair of wire cutters. Then remove the hook. Contact your vet; they may wish to prescribe antibiotics. Only your veterinarian should remove swallowed fishhooks.

Frostbite

Frostbite is skin damage as a result of cold. The skin will turn white if it is frostbitten. If it's severely frostbitten, the skin will actually turn black. Sometimes the affected skin will slough off, leaving a raw sore.

If the skin is white and intact, warm it slowly in tepid water (not hot—you can damage the skin further). It will be painful to warm the skin. In frostbite with sores, spread an antibiotic ointment on the area and wrap with gauze. In all cases of frostbite, seek veterinary attention.

Hypothermia

Dogs expend energy and heat while working, and insufficient food for a dog's energy requirements and dehydration can greatly affect your dog's ability to keep warm. If the heat loss is too great, your dog may experience hypothermia. Signs of hypothermia include lowered body temperature, shivering and lethargy, followed by stupor, shock, unconsciousness and finally, death.

Treatment for hypothermia is mostly common sense. Warm your dog slowly by wrapping her in blankets or lying next to her in blankets to help warm her. If she is conscious, offer her warm broth to drink. Seek immediate veterinary attention.

Heatstroke

Dehydration can occur during any season and may show up as weakness, extreme thirst and failure of the skin to snap back around the muzzle or neck. Signs of dehydration and heat stroke include elevated temperature, extreme thirst, watery diarrhea, vomiting, lethargy, high temperature (over 103°F), skin around the muzzle or neck that does not snap back when pinched, difficulty breathing, weakness and pale gums.

The onset of heatstroke is very sudden and sometimes it takes only a few minutes to reach an emergency situation. Blood pressure falls, mucous membranes turn icy blue, the dog becomes confused, staggers, is comatose and then dies.

Get the dog to someplace cool and shady. Pour cool water over her body and head or if possible, submerge her body in a tub or tank. Fan her and lift her coat with your fingers so that her skin will directly benefit from the cooling breeze and water. *Don't apply ice or ice water* because that will tend to close skin pores, shrink her skin's surface vessels and exacerbate the heatstroke.

When she comes around, give her small quantities of water to drink or pediatric electrolyte solution and repeat as often as she wants. If possible, measure her body temperature with a thermometer and stop the physical cooling process when her body reaches about 103 degrees, because the cooling will continue after you take her from the water and your target temperature is about 100 degrees.

The most common cause of heatstroke is leaving a dog in a car. Even with the windows cracked, the glass of the car magnifies the sun's temperature and the inside can easily reach 150 degrees even when the day is overcast and the outdoor temperature is moderate.

Insect Bites and Stings

You can treat most insect bites and stings with an over-the-counter antihistamine that your veterinarian can recommend. If your dog shows any allergic reaction to bites or stings, (severe swelling or difficulty breathing), seek immediate veterinary attention. This can be a life-threatening condition known as an anaphylactic shock.

Spider bites can be especially serious. The two most dangerous spiders are the black widow and the brown recluse. Both of these spider bites can be fatal if left untreated. If you suspect a spider has bitten your dog, seek immediate veterinary attention.

Poisoning

Contact your veterinarian or local poison control center and have available the substance or chemical that your dog ingested. Follow the veterinarian or poison control center's instructions. Do not induce vomiting unless told to do so. Some acids, alkalis and other substances can harm your dog more if they come back up.

CHAPTER 21

• •

THE SENIOR DOG

Nobody likes the thought of getting old, but there's no way to avoid it. The alternative is certainly more unpleasant! But what *is* old to a dog? And can you keep your dog active and healthy throughout his senior years?

ADOPTING A SENIOR MUTT

Why should you adopt a senior dog? Well, let's first determine what exactly a senior dog *is*. If you go to the animal shelter, the shelter might classify all dogs over five as seniors. Most dogs with good care can live past 10 years old (and maybe older), so senior doesn't sound that old, does it? This dog has half to two-thirds more of his life to live, if you'll adopt him.

But let's say the dog is older, perhaps eight or 10 years old. Why should you consider adopting such a dog? He's no longer the puppy who chews everything thing, knocks stuff over and has housebreaking accidents. He may not want to dash through the snow, but instead, he might enjoy snuggling up next to you on the couch by the fire.

Older dogs will tend to be more sedate, and most don't have the behavior problems you see in younger dogs. An older dog may know obedience commands.

Another reason is that if you really want to save a life, an older dog is less likely to be adopted. Puppies usually find homes, except in the most crowded of shelters; the older ones are the first to be put to death as "unadoptable." Older dogs may have been given up because their owners are deceased or couldn't care for them any longer.

Finally, I believe that the older dogs appreciate simple comforts. Most don't care anymore about dominance or pack status or chasing cats; they just want a bowl of food, a warm bed and someone to love them. Sounds ideal, doesn't it?

RECIPE FOR A LONG, HEALTHY LIFE

How old is "old" for a dog? It depends. Just as some people don't seem old even when they're in their 70s, some dogs don't seem old when other dogs are positively geriatric. Good genetics and a lifetime of exercise, good nutrition and medical care can make the difference.

Some dogs are seniors at seven years. This is especially true of mutts who have giant breeds, such as the Great Dane, in their mix. But some dogs can live to past 15 years old with good care. From eight to 10 years old, your dog will start showing more changes due to old age. After 10, I would call the dog a senior.

If your dog has been healthy and active, there's no reason he shouldn't continue being healthy and active just because he's older. In fact, if you start taking away his activities, you may find that he'll deteriorate faster.

Keep an eye on your dog when you work or exercise him, though. He may not be able to do everything a younger dog can, so don't insist on the same physical abilities you'd expect from a younger dog. But don't retire him yet either, unless he has a medical problem or an injury that rules out the activity. Some older dogs enjoy a scaled-down version of the sports they have always loved; it enables them to have fun and interact with you.

Feed your dog according to his weight and activity level. Don't necessarily switch him over to a "senior" diet unless he's gaining weight, his activity level has decreased or he has a physical condition that warrants a change in dog food. Many of my senior dogs still work and are active—and get premium performance dog food.

Don't be depressed that your dog is old—instead, enjoy him. Dogs can and do live healthy and physically active lives over the age of 10. I have two dogs who are 16 years old. Part of the credit for longevity goes to genetics, but part is also to medical care, diet and being physically active. You can't change genetics, but you can make a crucial difference in your dog's health and longevity.

KEEPING YOUR OLD DOG COMFORTABLE

Older dogs tend to enjoy a nice warm bed. Dogs who formerly eschewed the comforts of home will enjoy them now. A soft bed made from orthopedic foam can help relieve pressure points. Some pet equipment manufacturers have developed electric heating mats that radiate constant warmth for the dog. If you use one of these, be sure the cord is hidden so that your dog can't chew it and accidentally get a shock.

The stairs that were an obstacle back when your dog was a small puppy now may become a problem again. If you can, move his crate or bed to the lower floor of the house so that he doesn't have to climb stairs anymore, or install a ramp.

As your dog gets older, he may have trouble chewing his food. Moistening his dog food or feeding him canned food is an alternative that will help make him more comfortable. He may require trips to the doggy dentist for extra teeth cleaning and tooth extractions.

SENIOR HEALTH PROBLEMS

The normal process of aging makes every system in the body less efficient. Some dogs will experience minor losses in hearing and sight, some will lose more of their senses, some will develop diseases and some will just slow down a bit. Let's look at the more common health problems that can bother seniors.

Arthritis

Arthritis is fairly prevalent in older dogs. The onset of arthritis depends largely on how active your dog is. Couch potatoes are more likely to develop arthritis earlier than dogs who are physically active throughout their lives.

Luckily, there are several treatments available. Some supplements, such as glucosamine and MSM (found in Cosequin, Glycoflex and Synova-Cre), can help relieve the pain and slow the deterioration of arthritis. These supplements work well on some dogs and do nothing for others. Your dog usually has to be on them for more than six weeks before you can see any effect.

Your vet can help mitigate some of the effects of arthritis with anti-inflammatories such as NSAIDS (non-steroidal anti-inflammatory drugs). The downside to NSAIDS is some can adversely affect the kidneys and liver in some dogs. Dogs with sensitive stomachs can develop bleeding ulcers. Rimadyl, Metacam, Deramaxx and Zubrin are some of the NSAIDS available for veterinary use. Aspirin is a common pain reliever—but be sure ask your vet for the proper dosage. Do not give your dog either acetaminophen (Tylenol) or ibuprofen (Advil). They are poisonous to dogs.

Another potential weapon against arthritis is steroids. These can help bring relief and reduce inflammation, but they can have long-term drawbacks including immune-system suppression, increased appetite and weight, increased aggression and increased water consumption and urination.

Your vet can prescribe the right amount of buffered aspirin, anti-inflammatories or steroids to alleviate pain and swelling.

Blindness

You may not even notice at first if your dog goes blind. Most dogs are quite adept at getting around in familiar territory, even as their eyesight fails. The owner usually notices something is amiss when the dog bumps into an object that is out of place. Have your vet confirm your suspicions if you think your dog is blind.

Blind dogs require a little more care than sighted dogs. Don't rearrange the furniture. Keep a blind dog in familiar surroundings. Don't let him off the leash or he might wander around and become lost. When you're in an unfamiliar place, keep him beside you—you are his seeing-eye person now!

Cancer

Cancer and tumors are more prevalent with age. Cancer is the leading cause of death in dogs over eight years old. Although those numbers seem grim, *50 percent* of all cancers and tumors are curable. Cancer is not an automatic death sentence.

If you find a lump or bump that isn't normally on your dog, have it checked immediately. Some cancers and tumors are fast-spreading and if you wait too long, it may be too late for your veterinarian to do anything about them. Signs of cancer include abnormal growths, excessive weight loss, lack of appetite, bleeding, sores or wounds that will not heal, abnormal swellings, excessive sleep or lethargy, and difficulty breathing, eating or drinking.

Veterinarians use a combination of techniques to battle cancer. Surgery, chemotherapy and radiation have all been standard tools against cancer, but have now been significantly improved and are joined by other methods. Chemotherapy, long maligned for its side effects, now has been somewhat refined and is easier to handle. Researchers, using the latest DNA research, have developed certain drugs aimed specifically at the tumors and cancer, leaving healthy cells undamaged. Research being done on cancer vaccines may offer hope that someday a dog diagnosed with cancer can simply go in for a vaccination and have the body fight the cancer itself.

Cognitive Dysfunction Syndrome

Is your dog looking a little confused lately, or maybe acting a bit senile? Cognitive dysfunction syndrome does affect dogs, and is similar to Alzheimer's disease in humans. Dogs with this disease show a marked change in behavior. Your dog may suddenly look lost while standing in the middle of the room. He may not recognize loved ones and may forget his housetraining. His sleep may be disrupted and he may bark and carry on in the middle of the night.

The signs of a brain tumors may mimic cognitive dysfunction, so it is very important to have a brain tumor ruled out before treating cognitive dysfunction syndrome. The treatment of choice is Anipryl. The therapy can be expensive—$50 to $100 a month. Once the dog is on the therapy, he must remain on it his entire life or symptoms will reappear.

Congestive Heart Failure

Your dog may have congestive heart failure if he coughs or has respiratory distress, builds up fluid in the limbs and tires easily after even light exercise. There's no cure and it will ultimately be fatal, but it can be mitigated by diet and medication. You can help prevent congestive heart failure by keeping your dog active and fit. Obesity can contribute to or aggravate congestive heart failure.

Deafness

If your dog acts as if he's ignoring you, he may be going deaf. Deafness can come on gradually or suddenly. Clap your hands behind your dog's head or rattle the food bowl while he's in the other room. If he doesn't react, he's probably deaf. Your veterinarian can confirm your suspicions.

Deaf dogs can be exceedingly frustrating. You'll find yourself shouting at the dog for no good reason—as if a deaf dog will hear you if you talk louder. Some deaf dogs can hear whistles, but some are totally deaf.

If your dog is deaf, you'll have to teach him hand signals. I have one deaf dog in my house, and when I first started training him, I looked like a mime locked in the room with an angry bee. Start slowly—teach your dog as you would a puppy. It may take a little bit of time for him to pick up on what you want, but most dogs are pretty clever and figure us out in spite of ourselves.

You may be surprised to learn that there are hearing aids for dogs. These are still experimental, but some are available if you think your dog might benefit from one. Ask your veterinarian.

Dental Problems

Older dogs are more prone to dental problems because they tend to have worn or chipped teeth and tartar buildup. Bad breath, bleeding gums, loss of appetite, broken teeth or a buildup of brown tartar or plaque means the dog needs to go to the vet for a tooth cleaning and possible extraction. You can keep your dog's teeth healthy by brushing them often and giving him chews that help clean his teeth and gums.

Bladder and Kidney Problems

Signs of bladder or kidney problems include bloody or dark urine, more frequent drinking and urination, a hunched-up back and pain while urinating. Hard water, forcing a dog to hold it for long hours, and diet may contribute to urinary tract problems.

If your dog has blood in his urine or if he acts as though it is difficult to urinate, take him to your vet for an examination. Dogs, like people, can get kidney stones and bladder stones. If your dog has either, depending on his condition, your vet may prescribe a urine acidifier and antibiotics or may have to operate.

SHOULD YOU GET ANOTHER DOG?

As your dog ages, it might be tempting to get a puppy or another younger dog to help mitigate your sense of loss when your dog finally passes on. Should you do this? It depends.

Some dogs look on the newcomer as an interloper. A puppy or a new adult dog will take a large portion of your attention away from your current dog. If your dog is very old and is unable to keep up with the younger dog, he may resent the younger dog. The younger dog may become a bully because the older dog can't be physically active.

But there are cases where a younger dog and an older dog become fast friends. Suddenly, the older dog is playing like a puppy again and becomes the younger dog's aunt or uncle, happy to have a companion to play with.

Every dog is different, and it's impossible for me to say how your dog will react. Try having a friend with a young dog over for a canine play date, and see if you can gauge your dog's reaction.

SAYING GOOD-BYE

Saying good-bye is perhaps the hardest thing to do as a dog owner. I've had to put several of my dogs down now, and the truth is that it never gets any easier. Nor is the decision always clear.

Sometimes it's obvious: Your dog is in great pain and is dying from a terminal disease or injury. Other times, the diagnosis is unclear, or you're sitting in an emergency room and don't know what to do. Heroic efforts may be required to save him, which cost far beyond what you can afford, and your dog might have a very slim chance of recovery anyway. At times like this, talk to someone you can trust—perhaps your own vet, or you might obtain a second opinion. Other friends who are dog owners may be able to see clearly when you cannot. They may offer you advice that is not colored by the emotions of the situation.

When you're making this decision, ask yourself the following questions:

- Is your dog suffering?
- Will the proposed treatment improve the quality of life for your dog?
- Will the proposed treatment make a difference that will last longer than a few months?
- Can your dog enjoy life?
- Can your dog eat, breathe, urinate, defecate and move around easily?
- Can you afford the treatment?
- Are you keeping the dog alive for his sake or yours?

Don't allow your best friend to suffer needlessly. While it is tempting to try heroic measures to save your pet, you may discover that the result is still the same. Dogs don't live forever, and even though you want your dog to live a little longer, it may not be humane or even possible.

Euthanasia is painless and quick. The veterinarian will administer an injection and your pet will be gone. You can stay with your dog during his final minutes or leave—your choice. Many pet owners decide to stay with their dog during the last few minutes because it comforts the dog and brings closure.

You will grieve. This is normal and natural. Don't talk about it to people who don't have dogs because they may be the most callous. They may tell you the dog was "only a pet." No, he wasn't. Your dog was your friend and it would be strange to not grieve for a good friend who just died.

Talk to your vet about grief. They may be able to refer you to a free or low-cost pet loss counseling service. Many veterinary colleges and humane societies offer free or low-cost pet loss hotlines (see the box below). Take care of yourself during this time. Keep busy and active— exercise and eat a balanced diet. Avoid being alone and slipping into depression. You aren't denying that you have grief over the loss—you are helping yourself deal with it.

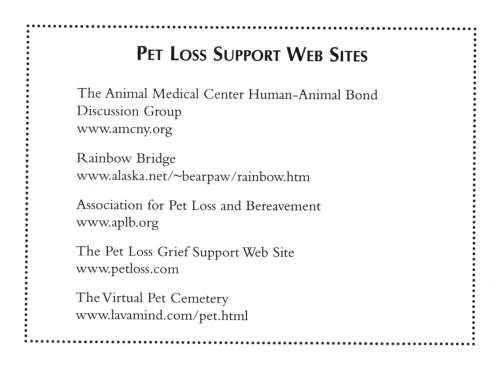

PET LOSS SUPPORT WEB SITES

The Animal Medical Center Human-Animal Bond
Discussion Group
www.amcny.org

Rainbow Bridge
www.alaska.net/~bearpaw/rainbow.htm

Association for Pet Loss and Bereavement
www.aplb.org

The Pet Loss Grief Support Web Site
www.petloss.com

The Virtual Pet Cemetery
www.lavamind.com/pet.html

THE RAINBOW BRIDGE

Just this side of heaven is a place called Rainbow Bridge.

When an animal dies that has been especially close to someone here, that pet goes to Rainbow Bridge. There are meadows and hills for all of our special friends so they can run and play together. There is plenty of food, water and sunshine, and our friends are warm and comfortable.

All the animals who had been ill and old are restored to health and vigor; those who were hurt or maimed are made whole and strong again, just as we remember them in our dreams of days and times gone by. The animals are happy and content, except for one small thing; they each miss someone very special to them, who had to be left behind.

They all run and play together, but the day comes when one suddenly stops and looks into the distance. His bright eyes are intent; His eager body quivers. Suddenly he begins to run from the group, flying over the green grass, his legs carrying him faster and faster.

You have been spotted, and when you and your special friend finally meet, you cling together in joyous reunion, never to be parted again. The happy kisses rain upon your face; your hands again caress the beloved head, and you look once more into the trusting eyes of your pet, so long gone from your life but never absent from your heart.

Then you cross Rainbow Bridge together. . . .

Author unknown

With time, the pain and anguish of your pet's death will fade. You will start remembering all the good times you had together. Perhaps, in time, you'll be ready to have another dog again. Perhaps you will get a puppy to keep yourself occupied. If you do, remember that no puppy will replace your beloved pet and that no dog will be like your departed dog. Your new puppy or dog will have a different personality and different behaviors. However, in time, you will grow to love this new addition as much as your beloved, departed pet.

THE LAST WORD

Mutts have touched the hearts of so many people throughout the ages, it's only fitting that there should be a book on them. I'll leave you with a story about Conan, my first mutt.

Conan was a black Newfoundland-Samoyed mix. He was stubborn and not very bright. Silly as it sounds, Conan became my first lead sled dog and helped me learn to mush with a three-dog team. We did pretty well our first year, taking fourth place at a couple of races.

But perhaps Conan shone the brightest during a particular emergency. We went mushing with some friends. One friend took off ahead of us and we waited for him to return. When he didn't, my husband, Larry, hooked up the team with Conan at lead.

Conan became all business, leading the four-dog team to our friend. Our friend had his sled but no dog team—the line had broken. Larry hooked the other sled to his and Conan led the team, towing both men and sleds back. Not once did Conan falter. We then drove to the other side of the trail and searched for the team. Eventually our friends found the dogs all alive, and only slightly the worse for wear (one had tangled with a porcupine).

I tell Conan's story because it is one of a mutt's courage. I could tell several other stories, but that would fill up another book: of Ed and Kersel, Skye, Cheyenne and other mutts whom I've have the privilege of working with. But those mutts are not the only great ones. There are other mutts out there showing great courage and performing miracles every day. And why not? A mutt's heart is as big as the world.

Rest in peace, Conan. You were a great friend.

Conan, my courageous mutt.

APPENDIX A

•••

USEFUL ORGANIZATIONS

AGILITY

Agility Association of Canada (AAC), RR #2, Lucan, Ontario, Canada, N0N2J0, (519) 657-7636, e-mail: www.aac.ca

Australian Shepherd Club of America (ASCA), 6091 East State Highway 21, Bryan, TX 77803-9652, (409) 778-1082, e-mail: www.asca.org

North American Dog Agility Council (NADAC), HCR 2, Box 277, St. Maries, ID 83861, (208) 689-3803, e-mail: www.nadac.com

United Kennel Club (UKC), 100 East Kilgore Road, Kalamazoo, MI 49001-5593, e-mail: www.ukcdogs.com

United States Dog Agility Association (USDAA), PO Box 850955, Richardson, TX 75085-0955, (888) AGILITY, e-mail: www.usdaa .com

CANINE GOOD CITIZEN

American Kennel Club, 5580 Centerview Drive, Raleigh, NC 27606-3390, (919) 233-9767, e-mail: www.akc.org

FLYBALL

North American Flyball Association, 1400 W. Devon Ave, #512, Chicago, IL 60660, (309) 688-9840, e-mail: www.flyball.org

FLYING DISC

Flying Disc Dog Open, Bill Watters/Director, P.O. Box 4615, Cave Creek, Arizona 85327, (888) 383-3357, (480) 595-0580 in Arizona, e-mail: www.airmajorsdoghouse.com/fddo/

National Canine Air Champions (NCAC), The Washington D.C. Area Frisbee Disc Dog Club, 2830 Meadow Lane, Falls Church, VA 22042, (703) 532-0709, e-mail: www.discdog.com

Skyhoundz, 4060 Peachtree Rd, Ste. D #326, Atlanta, GA 30319, (404) 256-4513 , e-mail: www.skyhoundz.com

FREESTYLE DANCING

Canine Freestyle Federation, Monica Patty, Corresponding Secretary, 21900 Foxden Lane, Leesburg, VA 20175, e-mail: www.canine-freestyle.org

World Canine Freestyle Organization, PO Box 250122, Brooklyn, NY 11235, (718) 332-8336, e-mail: worldcaninefreestyle.org

OBEDIENCE

American Mixed Breed Obedience Registration (AMBOR), 179 Niblick Rd. #113, Paso Robles, CA 93446, (805) 226-9275, e-mail: www.amborusa.org

Australian Shepherd Club of America (ASCA). *See* Agility.

Mixed Breed Dog Clubs of America (MBDCA), c/o Linda Lewis: Membership Secretary, 13884 State Route 104, Lucasville, OH 45648-8586, (740) 259-3941, e-mail: www.mbdca.org

United Kennel Club (UKC). *See* Agility.

THERAPY DOGS

Delta Society, 289 Perimeter Road East, Renton, WA 98055-1329, (425) 226-7357, e-mail: www.deltasociety.org

Therapy Dogs International, Attn: New Registrations, 88 Bartley Road, Flanders, NJ 07836, (973) 252-9800, e-mail: www.tdi-dog.org

HOLISTIC VETERINARY MEDICINE

American Holistic Veterinary Medical Association, 2214 Old Emmorton Road, Bel Air, MD 21015, (410) 569-0795, e-mail: www.ahvma.org

American Veterinary Chiropractic Association, PO Box 249, Port Byron, IL 61275, (309) 523-3995, e-mail: www.animalchiropractic.org

International Veterinary Acupuncture Society (IVAS), PO Box 1478, Longmont, CO 80534, (303) 682-1167, e-mail: www.ivas.org

National Center for Homeopathy, 801 N. Fairfax #306, Alexandria, VA 22314, (703) 548-7790, e-mail: www.homeopathic.org

PET HEALTH INSURANCE

Pet Assure, 10 South Morris St., Dover, NJ 07801, (888) 789-PETS, e-mail: www.petassure.com

PetCare Insurance Programs, PO Box 8575, Rolling Meadows, IL 60008-8575, (866) 275-PETS, e-mail: www.petcareinsurance.com/us/

Pet Plan Insurance, 777 Portage Ave, Winnipeg, MB, Canada, R3G0N3, (905) 279-7190, e-mail: www.petplan.com

Petshealth Insurance Agency, PO Box 2847, Canton, OH 44720, (888) 592-7387, e-mail: www.petshealthplan.com

Premier Pet Insurance Group, 9541 Harding Blvd, Wauwatosa, WI 53226, (877) 774-2273, e-mail: www.ppins.com

Veterinary Pet Insurance (VPI), PO Box 2344, Brea, CA 92822-2344, (800) USA-PETS, e-mail: www.petinsurance.com

ANIMAL REGISTRY AND RECOVERY

AKC Companion Animal Recovery, 5580 Centerview Drive, Suite 250, Raleigh, NC 27606-3389, (800) 252-7894, e-mail: www.akccar.org

National Dog Registry, Box 116, Woodstock, NY 12498, (800) 637-3647, e-mail: www.natldogregistry.com

Tattoo-A-Pet, 6571 S.W. 20th Court, Ft. Lauderdale, FL 33317, (800) 828-8667, e-mail: www.tattoo-a-pet.com

VETERINARY ASSOCIATIONS

American Animal Hospital Association (AAHA), PO Box 150899, Denver, CO 80215-0899, e-mail: www.aahanet.org

American College of Veterinary Internal Medicine, 1997 Wadsworth Blvd, Suite A, Lakewood, CO 80215-3327, e-mail: www.acvim.org

American Veterinary Medical Association, 1931 N. Meacham Rd, Suite 100, Schaumburg, IL 60173-4360, (847) 925-8070, e-mail: www.avma.org

TATTOO REGISTRIES

National Dog Registry, Box 116, Woodstock, NY 12498, (800) 637-3647, e-mail: www.natldogregistry.com

Tattoo-A-Pet, 6571 S.W. 20th Court, Ft. Lauderdale, FL 33317, (800) 828-8667, e-mail: www.tattoo-a-pet.com

MICROCHIP REGISTRIES

AKC Companion Animal Recovery, 5580 Centerview Drive, Suite 250, Raleigh, NC 27606-3389, (800) 252-7894, e-mail: www.akccar.org

Identichip, 4894 Lone Mountain Road, PMB 169, Las Vegas, NV 89130, (800) 926-1313, e-mail: www.identichip.com

InfoPET, 415 West Travelers Trail, Burnsville, MN 55337, (800) INFO-PET

PetNet, 620 Alden Road, Suite 101, Markham, Ontario, Canada, L3R9R7, (905) 477-6950, e-mail: www.petnet.ca

PETtrac, 3179 Hammer Ave., Norco, CA 91760, (800) 336-AVID, e-mail: www.avidmicrochip.com

APPENDIX B

MORE READING

PERIODICALS

AKC Gazette, 51 Madison Ave, New York, NY 10010

Dog Fancy, P.O. Box 53264, Boulder, CO 80322-3264
(800) 365-4421, e-mail: www.dogfancy.com

Dog World, P.O. Box 56240, Boulder, CO 80323-6240, (800) 361-8056

BOOKS

Alderton, David, *The Dog Care Manual,* Barron's Educational Series, 1986.

American Kennel Club, *The Complete Dog Book, 19th Edition Revised,* Howell Book House, 1997.

Benjamin, Carol Lea, *Second-Hand Dog,* Howell Book House, 1988.

Bonham, Margaret H. and Wingert, James M., DVM, *The Complete Idiot's Guide to Dog Health and Nutrition,* Alpha Books, 2003.

Bonham, Margaret H., *An Introduction to Dog Agility,* Barron's Educational Series, 2000.

Bonham, Margaret H., *The Simple Guide to Getting Active with Your Dog,* TFH Publications, 2002.

Coffman, Howard D., *The Dry Dog Food Reference,* Pig Dog Press, 1995.

Derrico, Karen, and McElroy, Susan Chernak, *Unforgettable Mutts: Pure of Heart Not of Breed,* NewSage Press, 1999.

Fogle, Bruce, DVM, *The New Encyclopedia of the Dog,* Dorling Kindersley, 2000.

Giffin, James M., MD, and Carlson, Liisa D., DVM, *The Dog Owner's Home Veterinary Handbook, 3rd edition,* Howell Book House, 2000.

James, Ruth B., DVM, *The Dog Repair Book,* Alpine Press, 1990.

Klever, Ulrich, *The Complete Book of Dog Care,* Barron's Educational Series, 1989.

LaBelle, Charlene, *A Guide to Backpacking with Your Dog,* Alpine Publications, 1993.

Streitferdt, Uwe, *Healthy Dog, Happy Dog,* Barron's Educational Series, 1994.

Volhard, Joachim, Volhard Wendy, Volhard, Jack, *The Canine Good Citizen: Every Dog Can Be One,* Howell Book House, 1997.

Zink, M. Chris, DVM, PhD, *Peak Performance, Coaching the Canine Athlete,* Howell Book House, 1992.

INDEX